The Transformational Entrepreneur:

Creating a Life of Dedication and Service

Other Titles by Connie Ragen Green

Living the Internet Lifestyle: Quit Your Job, Become an Entrepreneur, and Live Your Ideal Life

The Weekend Marketer: Say Goodbye to the '9 to 5', Build an Online Business, and Live the Life You Love

Time Management Strategies for Entrepreneurs: How to Manage Your Time to Increase Your Bottom Line

The Inner Game of Internet Marketing

Membership Sites Made Simple: Start Your Own Membership Site for Passive Online Income

Article Marketing: How to Attract New Prospects, Create Products, and Increase Your Income

Targeted Traffic Techniques for Affiliate Marketers

Huge Profits with Affiliate Marketing: How to Build an Online Empire by Recommending What You Love

Huge Profits with a Tiny List: 50 Ways to Use Relationship Marketing to Increase Your Bottom Line

The Transformational Entrepreneur:

Creating a Life of Dedication and Service

By
Connie Ragen Green

Copyright © 2014 by Hunter's Moon Publishing
ISBN: 978-1-937988-12-8

Hunter's Moon Publishing
http://HuntersMoonPublishing.com

Interior Design by Geoff Hoff
Cover Design by Shawn Hansen

Dedication

This book is dedicated to two women who grace my life by living a life they love and showing me what is possible when you put your heart, mind, and soul into everything you do.

One is Allison Mason, a talented and creative stylist I have been working with since 2007. Allison is a beautiful human being inside and out who has been a cheerleader in my personal quest to become an author, speaker and an entrepreneur all along my journey. She has listened to me drone on endlessly about my business, asked probing questions and shared insights in a way that makes me think. She continues to give me confidence, as she has from the very beginning by working her magic on me so that I would indeed be ready for my close-up. Thank you for being a special person in my life, Alli.

The other is Brittany Little, someone who came into my life at just the perfect time. She is a wife, a mother, a sister, a daughter, and an incredible friend to me and to so many others. Brittany has been a reminder that strong women can also be compassionate, loving, and kind. She has been there for my family in so many ways and during times when I could not be there myself, helping them in their own life's journey. She radiates excellence in everything she does and seems to have boundless energy and ideas as to how to make everyone in her life feel more special and loved every single day. Thank you from the bottom of my heart, Brittany.

Table of Contents

Foreword

I was initially introduced to Connie during the summer of 1987. Mutual friends thought we should meet because we were each involved in real estate and could possibly do some business together. They told me she was a new classroom teacher who had decided not to give up her real estate career once she had earned her teaching credential. I was intrigued by her story and agreed to the meeting.

We were to meet in front of a local restaurant after school one day. She was teaching at a year round school that began on July 1 each year, so we decided to meet for an early dinner. I can remember like it was yesterday seeing her car pull into the driveway of the restaurant's parking lot. She was driving a Japanese car, a little brown coupe, and her eyes became wide as saucers when she spotted me. I would later tease her like she looked like a deer in the headlights at that moment.

If you've ever met Connie you know that she is instantly likeable. She smiles and makes eye contact and has a way about her that puts you at ease. What I would find out later was that she is also sizing up the person she meets and thinking about how she can be of service to them in the future. Quite a remarkable trait that I have seldom observed in others during my lifetime.

As we ate dinner, Connie talked about her work as a teacher. My children were quite young at that time and I remember thinking they would be lucky to have a teacher like Mrs. Green one day. She also shared her love of real estate, and that she believed she felt drawn to helping people purchase homes because she had grown up in poverty. She and her mother had never owned a house. Once she became an adult she made it her mission to become a property owner as soon as possible and had achieved this while still in college. I was quite impressed. My own family was well off and I had not given a second thought to buying my own home until I was almost thirty.

Connie became a family friend, and quickly made it to the 'short list' of adults my children wanted to spend time with. My wife was happy I had someone to 'play' real estate with, and we began to look at a variety of investments that would make sense for both of us. Even back then she had the entrepreneurial spirit and taking risks was never something she feared or avoided. In fact, she was positively fearless when it came to facing most anything in her life. This impressed me to no end.

The most remarkable thing Connie took on back in the 1990s was to gather a group of us and convince us that we should purchase an apartment building together as a Limited Partnership LLC. She had located a distressed property in an area that had once been extremely popular. It was a fifty-seven unit building that would require updating and renovation if it were to become a good rental building.

Using her sixth sense, or so it seemed, she presented us with a laundry list of reasons why this area was sure to rebound in the near future and why this purchase would change all of our lives.

It took many years for this to happen, but Connie refused to give up. Many of us were ready to walk away from our investment at various times, such as after the Northridge earthquake in 1993 and when rent control became the law in Los Angeles. She singlehandedly kept our group of ten men and one woman together, and sure enough things began to turn around and work out exactly as she had said they would. Given the fact that she went through cancer treatment during this time, was building her own real estate business, while also succeeding in the classroom this was no small feat.

If you have the opportunity to spend time with Connie, do it at any cost. She is honest, caring, and oh so smart. Her insight is uncanny, her wisdom far beyond her years, and her compassion for others unmatched. Connie Ragen Green is, in my humble opinion, a force to be reckoned with and someone you want to know.

Everett Mitchell
September 2, 2014
Los Angeles, California

Connie Ragen Green Always Delivers

I always warn my customers about Connie Ragen Green. Sure she seems like a sweet, grand-motherly (but not old!) type woman. Yes, you'd likely find her running some sort of civically responsible social event. Yes, it's true she was a school teacher.

However – she's also a closer. I tell my clients that if you get in a room with her and she's speaking, you'll likely be buying it. That woman can sell!

I first met Connie at a seminar in back in 2009, I believe. I liked her instantly. Warm, compassionate, caring. All that jazz. Underneath it though, I could see she had an approach of resolve... she doesn't quit. One of the things that motivates her, I'm sure, is the solutions she offers to her customers are so helpful... she feels compelled to get them to her customers.

The only thing I can think of that's "changed" about Connie since I first met her – she has just continued to set her sights on larger and more powerful goals. Which is inevitable when you're someone like Connie – because that's the type of person who strives to do their best not to beat someone else, but to contribute more than last year... and the year before and the year before. And the next year it's the same thing.

While most entrepreneurs I know have changed for the worst – meaning they weren't able to stay on top of servicing their customers because that didn't have the focus and resolve – Connie continues to deliver.

This, of course, extends far beyond business. Connie is one of the most charitable people I know because she contributes not just with money but with her time to create both a better community locally and globally. I can say I'm honored to call her a friend and it'll be exciting to watch her transform even further in the years to come.

Jason Fladlien
September 4, 2014

Preface

First of all, thank you for taking the time to read this book. With so many titles to choose from, authors know that you have a vast choice when it comes to reading. I appreciate that you were at least intrigued enough by the title and the cover of my book to make it to this page. Please indulge me now as I share with you how and why this book came to be, and why I believe your life will be forever changed once you've read, internalized, and acted upon the concepts and ideas I share here.

In the spring of 2005 I awoke to a feeling of intense desire for change in my life. It had been coming for some time, years perhaps, but on this day the feeling was so strong I simply could not ignore it any longer. It was as though I was seeing the world through new eyes. Even though I got dressed and went to work that day, something deep inside of me had changed forever and I knew I would not be able to push down this internal emotion for even one more day. Something deep inside of me was yearning to be released, and on that day I finally acknowledged it.

I must explain that at this time I was working as a classroom teacher in the Los Angeles area. In my 'spare time', which is quite a play on words if you know anyone who teaches, I worked as a real estate broker and residential appraiser. This meant that I arose each morning around four-thirty, left my home before six, and did not return home again until eight or nine in the evening. I did this six or seven days a week, simply so I could make ends meet and have some semblance of a good life within my means. This had gone on for most of the previous twenty years.

I was not unhappy, or even dissatisfied with my life at that time. It was just that everything had become more challenging and more complicated as I had become a little older. In 1992 I had cancer for the first time at the age of thirty-seven, and the doctors did not expect for me to survive. The cancer recurred several years later, and simultaneously I was dealing with a work related injury that required me to have rotator cuff surgery on my shoulder and knee surgery to repair a torn meniscus within a few months of each other. Suddenly, my life as a classroom teacher by day and a road warrior in the real estate world at night and on the weekends was not an easy one.

That summer I would be turning fifty years old, and I believe the events that came after that day were all part of a self-imposed midlife crisis that would end up being the most important time of my life. This was my prayer:

Dear God, please show me a way to work from home, from my bedroom if necessary, so that I can earn enough income to meet all of my financial obligations with grace and ease.

As soon as I voiced this desire to myself and to the people around me all those years ago a flood of resources came my way. This included randomly meeting a couple who invited me to visit their church (the renowned Agape Center in Los Angeles) and recommending a number of books for me to read. Overnight it seemed like the universe heard my cry and came forth in a massive way to guide me through the steps necessary to change my present situation into one more to my liking. When the student (me) was ready, many teachers appeared.

During the next twelve months I made the conscious decision to change my life completely. I resigned from the school district, gave away my best real estate clients, and pursued a course of study that would lead me to starting my own online business. I needed to make room for the new opportunities and challenges that were presenting themselves to me on an almost daily basis during that time.

What has occurred in my life since this time is nothing short of a radical and miraculous transformation, and I feel compelled to share every step of this journey with you. My transformation came about once I was willing to deconstruct every belief I had and open my mind to even greater possibilities than I had ever dreamed at any time in my life before now.

My goal in this work is to include you in this journey from this day forward. No matter what you are doing now, I want you to know you can create a life of your choosing over the next year or so. I will share my favorite saying with you here:

> *"Live for a year the way others won't; live the rest of your life the way others can't."*

This continues to be my experience and I want it to be yours as well, if that is your desire.

May your journey be a satisfying and joyous one, and as you get nearer to your destination may you realize that it has all unfolded in exactly the way it should have and makes perfect sense.

Connie Ragen Green
September 7, 2014
Santa Barbara, California

Introduction

"Perhaps the very best question that you can memorize and repeat, over and over, is, "What is the most valuable use of my time right now?"
~Brian Tracy

It is my sincere hope that this book will be the one that changes your life. My goal is to grab your attention and intensify your desire to know more and begin taking action. That said, my intention is to get inside of your head and make you think. If I accomplish that, then my mission will be accomplished.

The true purpose of this book is to address the four 'big' questions in regards to entrepreneurial transformation and to take you step by step through the process of inducing your own transformation, one day and one thought at a time.

Section I answers the question of exactly what transformation is and how to recognize when the time is right for you to think about, plan, and take action with this renewal to benefit your own life. I provide a series of examples to further enhance your thinking on this topic in a way that can be applied to your current situation

Section II moves on to the idea of why we should even care about the transformational process, specifically in regards to entrepreneurs. This is where you will explore your own unique thoughts and opinions on this matter, placing you in a superior position to define the paradigm that will make the most sense for you if you choose to carry on and follow through with my suggestions.

In Section III we delve into the concepts around the 'what if?' of transformation, and I go into great detail as to the age old question of whether it is the journey or the destination that matters most in your life.

Section IV teaches how you can begin your transformation today. I use my own life as a model and an example, as I would never ask you to embark on a journey that I, myself have not taken.

I outline a Blueprint for Transformation in Section V. Even though entrepreneurs tend to shy away from this type of structure, I felt it important enough that I created an entire section that will serve to guide you on your way to your destination, one none of us will ever reach if we continue to pursue true transformation.

My primary intention here is to focus exclusively on making the life journey an even more joyous one than it has been up until this time, and to explain in great detail why I believe the *destination* is the most important piece of your journey.

I've long since come to the realization and belief that true transformation must begin deep inside of you when that first seed of hope is planted. For me, this originally occurred when I made the conscious decision in April of 2005 to change my life completely, which included my desire to find a way to replace my current income with a home-based business.

Within a year I had walked away from my job as a classroom teacher and given away my real estate clients.

The idea of being able to work from my home and earn enough income to replace what had previously taken me ten to fourteen hours a day away from home was a dream that I was willing to work for in order to realize and manifest. It took me about eighteen months to achieve this goal, and the journey was one I would not trade for anything now.

My next challenge was to help others who were searching for a different way of living to transform their financial life in a similar way. I knew that many people were dreaming of quitting a job that no longer served them and working from home in a way that fit their lifestyle and needs.

The thought that any one person in business could transform, influence, or persuade another to take actions leading to universal change is a lofty one, yet I've witnessed this type of occurrence over and over since starting my own online business in 2006.

Additionally, this book is intended as an exploration of the human condition, wherein you as the reader will have the opportunity to dig deep in an effort to bring about and facilitate real change in one or more areas of your life. If you are willing to accept this challenge be aware that it will most likely be a painful one in the beginning, as you discover things about yourself that you may not even have suspected have been there all along.

However, when you are courageous enough to step into this realm, a parallel universe of sorts, the world opens up in a way that people far more intelligent than me have yet to be able to put into words. It's a feeling of love and joy and well-being, and it is most definitely worth your time and effort to put one foot in front of the other and begin your own journey.

What this book is definitely *NOT* about is the idea that you can and should change people who have no desire or yearning to change. Start with your own transformation, become an excellent role model to the people around you, and then stand back and watch as those you care about the most begin their own process.

To Your Transformation,
Connie Ragen Green

Section I

What is Transformation?

"Do not go where the path may lead, go instead where
there is no path and leave a trail."
~ Ralph Waldo Emerson

To fully explore the topic of transformation and all that it implies, it is first necessary to take at least a short journey into defining exactly what its meaning is to me and can be to you.

I'll define transformation, as I am referring to it within the confines of this book as meaning a total and complete change in regards to body, mind, and spirit that is initiated when one feels the longing to move away from their current situation and on to one that will be more fulfilling, satisfying, and closer to the Core Values they were born with.

Radical or revolutionary transformation consists of a thorough or dramatic change in form or appearance. It's an alteration, mutation, conversion, metamorphosis, transfiguration, or transmutation of what was originally in place.

Of course, there is even more to it than this so please bear with me as I get into the concepts, strategies, and possible outcomes this type of change can bring in your life and in the lives of those around you.

Transformation in regards to entrepreneurism involves taking all of this information and these concepts one step further into your working and creative life as you do business and interact with other entrepreneurs and small businesses over the course of your lifetime. Being aware that you are operating on this level lays you wide open to enjoying the best of everything life has to offer in terms of physical, emotional, and financial rewards.

The connotation that has been more typically associated with the idea of transformation is change at the basic and uninspired level, something we all fear to some extent and do not seek out. Change for the sake of changing has little value, and is tantamount to changing the color of your shirt and socks each day. What I am talking about here is digging deep down into your Core and consciously working towards inspired and meaningful change.

I knew that I was in for some hard work if I were to commit to this undertaking in my own life, and I could feel my chest tighten each time I thought about what could be ahead. I finally made the decision to plunge in head first and face whatever lay ahead in a positive and cheerful way. Once I had reminded myself that the level of transformation I was seeking was very different, it was a simple action to move forward.

Transformation As Growth

We have all transformed multiple times in our lives already, whether these changes were conscious and premeditated or not. Desiring to go in another direction leads to transformation every time. Is it not transformational when we choose to go to college rather than take a job, take an apartment instead of remaining in our parent's home, or get married rather than continuing to date?

Yet, in each of the scenarios I have described here we may have felt as though these were simply rites of passage at certain stages of our lives. We may have been following the crowd or doing what was suggested to us by someone we respected, or even feared at the core level.

The path of finishing high school, going on to college, meeting a partner, moving into your own living space, taking a job, getting married, buying a home, and on and on is transformation on an unconscious level, in my honest opinion.

We must take the full responsibility for experiencing change and growth in our lives that will lead us in the direction of joy, happiness, satisfaction, and a feeling of living up to our full potential instead of just doing what others around us are doing.

You will benefit from reading about my own experiences with the concepts I am describing here, and I will share with you that when I was fifteen years old I saved up for a Schwinn Continental ten speed bicycle because everyone I was friends with at the time had one. It was bright canary yellow with very skinny, smooth low-friction tires, racing handlebars that curved under so you were completely bent over the frame while you rode, and a seat so tiny only your tail bone was supported.

It only took a few hours before I admitted to myself that I hated riding this bicycle. Instead of allowing myself to choose a bike that I would enjoy I was influenced by 'group think' and made a decision that brought me no joy or enjoyment at all.

I promised myself right then and there that I would never get caught up in this behavior again, and have done very well since this event back in 1970 to do just that. What is your memory of allowing someone else's ideas influence your behavior?

Now you might be thinking that I did transform and grow as a result of this experience, and you would be correct, but I will argue that we do not need to learn our lessons the hard way in order to change our lives and move in the direction that will serve us best over the course of our lifetime.

Continuing to remodel and morph from the person you are today into the person you were meant to be is a natural progression. While I was teaching in the classroom my students continually felt bad because they were not already the person they wanted to become. I began then to teach them that we are all in 'the process of becoming' the person we will finally be, and that it will be this way until the day we die. This seemed to make them more patient about their own situation and I now teach this to adults I mentor, friends and family members, and audiences I address all over the world. Allow yourself the time to know what it is that you want in your life, and then go after it in a way and in the time frame that works best for you.

Must You Transform To Achieve Success?

At this point in your reading you may be thinking that you do not need to transform or change or morph into someone else in order to be successful. I believe the opposite, but let's discuss this way of thinking for a moment.

Change is not a simple undertaking for any of us. In fact, our history as human beings includes the ability to resist change as long as possible for self-preservation, and to only adapt to change when no other course of action is possible. However, as modern, upwardly mobile humans we have the choice to stick with the status quo, and its results or to choose to change in a way that suits our personality and lifestyle goals.

Think back to when you were in high school or college. During this time you more than likely had your own preconceived ideas about what your life would be like. Perhaps professional sports or a career in the arts struck your fancy. Why didn't you achieve your lofty goal? Probably because you were not willing to make the sacrifices necessary to reach the results you were dreaming of. You were unwilling to change.

I wanted to write screenplays and situation comedies for television, yet I was unwilling to change my habits to those of a published writer. I also wanted to be a veterinarian, but was unwilling to do whatever it would take to complete the required coursework in science and mathematics at the college level.

What did you miss out on because you clung to stagnation and what was familiar and comfortable in your life at that time? Do you still know anyone from those days who changed their mind, attitude, and habits and achieved their dreams? I do. One is a screenwriter and the other is a veterinarian.

These people are just two examples of the ones I have known over my lifetime who were committed to and disciplined enough to follow through with their goals. You may have heard that if someone is interested in something they will do what is convenient to achieve it, but if they are committed they will do *whatever it takes* to get to the finish line. I want you to travel on the journey of being fully devoted, dedicated, and committed to achieving your goals. Are you in?

The Role of Thought Leaders

Thought leaders can be described as trusted individuals who move and inspire people with their creative and innovative ideas. A thought leader can turn their ideas into reality, many times with the help of other thought leaders, or even with people who simply have a simple idea they would like to see brought to fruition.

Typically they will create a dedicated group of friends and followers into a type of group Mastermind. This enables them to scale their ideas into lasting change. Many times these evolutionary, or even revolutionary ideas change the world forever in a meaningful way and compel the rest of us to be open to new ways of thinking by codifying the steps to success and creating a foundation for others to build upon. In my world of online marketing people like Steve Jobs and Bill Gates come to mind as thought leaders that have made it possible for me to have the life I now lead.

In 2008 I joined a Mastermind, one that was led by and included several thought leaders. This was my first foray into this world, and now I can't imagine how I ever survived without surrounding myself with these people. Just the idea of having extremely smart, gifted, and understanding people listen to my ideas and share their own experiences with me was an amazing one.

I would encourage you to think of the people you consider to be thought leaders and begin reading their books, meeting them in person, and following their ideas as a way to begin your own life transformation. Then join or form your own group to immerse yourself with innovative thoughts and ideas.

Change Your Mind...
Change Your Life

When I think back to my life up to the age of fifty it is difficult for me to believe the person in my memory was actually me. I have gone through such a dramatic renewal and morphing during these past few years that I am almost unrecognizable to myself.

Now I am not talking about a physical or cosmetic transformation, even though you may be thinking that dropping a few pounds and changing your hairstyle may be a desirable and welcomed change. No, that is too shallow a way of thinking about all of this that is possible in your life.

Instead, I am talking here about a multi-layered transformation that shakes you to your core and allows you to change at the cellular level.

What does this mean, exactly?

The meaning behind this type of thinking goes deep into your soul. I firmly believe that we live our lives in a fog much of the time, not sure what to do next or which road to pursue and just trying to avoid doing the wrong thing that will lead us down a path of no return. We use less than ten percent of our brain capacity. It doesn't have to be this way.

Instead, I want you to think about being fully conscious and aware of every detail of every day and part of your life. Know that you truly cannot make the wrong decision in any aspect of your life, as long as you take the time to check in with yourself regularly. Let me give you some examples of this in action.

While I was a classroom teacher at four different schools over a twenty year period I was constantly at odds with the administration and even some of the other teachers. Just thinking about this now again proves to me that I have become a completely different person from the one I was back then.

Every day I was in what I refer to as 'reactionary mode', meaning that everything that happened throughout the day was something that I thought of as 'happening to me', rather than occurring to all of the parties involved. This supposes that I was always the victim of unkind words and actions from others around me, decisions that were made that did not please me, and situations that made me extremely uncomfortable.

I now know that I was definitely not a victim at any time, and that is was simply my lack of initiative in taking and assuming full responsibility for what was happening around me that was to blame. That's correct, if you are not taking responsibility for each and every occurrence in your life, you have only yourself to blame.

Herein lies the Challenge to many. I have also learned and come to accept the fact that transformation will not be so easy for everyone, and that part of my own journey is to step back from what I am able to achieve and reach out to those who seek greater clarity and strength to transform their own lives. For it is not for me to judge anyone, even myself, but far more important to help facilitate change in those who seek this as a part of their own life experience.

How Does This Relate To Entrepreneurship?

Because this book deals with transformation as it applies to entrepreneurs, we will now get to the heart of the matter and the reason I wrote this book to begin with.

Entrepreneurs are very different from other people in that they are willing to accept and assume a level of risk that is simply not required of the remainder of the population on our planet.

Real World Examples of Transformational Entrepreneurship

I have never been one to rely exclusively upon theory when it comes to building the infrastructure of my life and business. For this reason I thought it important to include some pertinent details of how other groups, organizations, and entrepreneurs bring the concept of transformation into their workplaces.

The example I wish to share is from one of the largest and most innovative companies on the planet. Google is a search engine giant that allows its people to spend twenty percent of their time working on a 'pet' project that appeals to them. This simple concept allows people to do what they are interested in and as a result they become significantly more productive. I love that, don't you?

This policy has continued to work so well at Google's headquarters that at least 50% of their most popular projects are said to have been created during this time. Creative thinking leads to innovations and 'out of the box' thinking that can change the world one step at a time. Gmail, Google News, and other ideas were first created as ideas the engineers were passionate about and were able to more fully develop as projects during this 20% time of their work week.

This is implemented using something called the 'Genius Hour'. This concept emerged not too many years ago in some of the world's most innovative organizations, including Google. It was originally inspired by founders Sergey Brin and Larry Page, based on their Montessori School experience as children. I was also a Montessori kid, so this idea of discovery and self exploration as a part of structured business makes perfect sense to me.

Google, as well as the leaders of several other companies invited their employees to explore their own ideas for contributing to the success of the organization, something that had rarely been done in the past.

It became a philosophy and even a policy that every employee working at Google spend about twenty percent of their time working on ideas and projects that interest that employee. This is equivalent to one full work day each week. They're encouraged to explore anything other than what they would normally be working on as a part of their job. As a result, 50% of all of Google's products developed by 2009 originated from this 20% free time, including Gmail. Real break-through happens when we are free from others' expectations and driven by individual passion.

When the leaders finally recognized and acknowledged they needed to change up what they had been doing for so long, the people working for them were able to think differently and come up with some brilliant and creative ideas. The idea was to disrupt the status quo and trust the employees to come up with something useful.

The result was a Genius Hour, which gives them time each week to work on new ideas, to master new skills, or to simply brainstorm what could be possible. It may not sound like very much time, but the results have been nothing short of remarkable.

Google did not originate the idea of giving employees the time to explore and discover new ideas, passions, and outcomes. The 3M Company, headed up by William Coyne during the 90s, gave his teams free reign to work for extended periods of time on their own with little or no interference from anyone else. He explained that

> *"After you plant a seed in the ground, you don't dig it up every week to see how it is doing."*

This discussion of the Genius Hour and allowing workers to engage in creative thoughts and actions for twenty percent of their work time brings us now to a discussion of something known as the 80/20 Law. I have written about this more extensively in two of my previous books, and will share with you that this concept is responsible for much of my success during the past nine years.

This law states that twenty percent of what you do will account for eighty percent of your results. If you think about this in your own life experience you will understand immediately what this means.

You may ask twenty of your friends and neighbors to help you set up the backyard for a party or celebration of some kind. Typically, it will be three, four, or five people who come forward to do so. You may be asked to go somewhere to eat with friends or co-workers, and there is usually about a twenty percent chance you will follow through and join them.

In business this translates to seeing eighty percent of your results from about twenty percent of the actions you take. Once you can identify which actions are the most effective you will increase your productivity and thus, your bottom line.

Traits of a Transformational Entrepreneur

Did you know that entrepreneurs tend to sleep fewer hours that most other people? Numerous studies have validated this to be true, and perhaps it is because entrepreneurs always feel like there is more to be accomplished each day than the average person might believe is so.

Entrepreneurs are risk takers. We are willing to work for extended periods of time without earning any income at all, thereby honing our vision before revealing it to the world. This can be difficult at best, with family members and close friends worrying that we have lost our minds, or at least our ability to reason.

Being an observer and student of human behavior I love to connect with entrepreneurs, both new and seasoned ones, to compare notes on what goes through our mind when we decide to commit to a new project. It becomes an obsession with us to work on it until it is finished or until we can no longer justify the viability of our idea, at which point we allow it to die a slow death.

Section II

Why Do We Care About Transformation?

"Don't wait; the time will never be just right."
~Napoleon Hill

Now that you know exactly what I am referring to when I talk about transformation on both a personal and professional level, you may be wondering why we care about this. It's an excellent question that we will explore in more detail here and throughout the remainder of this book.

There are several reasons why anyone would care about making a transformation to their life and/or to their business.

The first reason may arise from the realization that what you are doing no longer serves you in the way it once did. For example, when I became a teacher back in the 1980s I was excited at the possibilities of working with children and expanding their horizons through formal education and experiences. After fifteen years of working in the classroom with children aged five to eighteen I became disillusioned with the process and with the system. I felt that I was just going through the paces each day without having a true connection to what I was doing and saying any longer. I longed for a way to reconnect with the children and my fellow teachers in a way that would be rewarding and satisfying. When I did not find that I made the decision to leave teaching altogether in pursuit of other opportunities and experiences.

Another reason one desires to make a dramatic and radical change to their life is based on a specific experience they may have in their life. I have witnesses people waking up one day and feeling like they were living the wrong life for them.

Part of this involves wanting to do your best in every endeavor you undertake. My friend, author and actress Marilu Henner, has proclaimed this to be her year of doing her personal best. I love this idea because it is an internal growth not based on competition from the outside world.

"The only person you should try to be better than…is the person you were yesterday."

Transformation supposes, no, it actually requires, no, it most definitely demands that you take an honest look at who you are and who you want to be.

During the twenty years that I worked as a classroom teacher, while also working in real estate in my 'spare' time, I would have to admit that seldom did I actually do my best. I did what was required and expected of me, and many times I went above and beyond when it came to helping the children, but I never did my best on a consistent basis. Looking back, I'm not sure how I was able to go about each day by acting in such a minimal way.

I can actually remember the time when I made the conscious decision to do my best every single day. It was in the spring of 2004, at a time when I realized I did not want to be a teacher any longer. I decided to pretend my job with the school district paid me a million dollars a year, and went about each day doing what a person earning that amount of income would do. This was based on reading I had done that said we must fully appreciate what we currently have in our life if we expect to get more.

It was funny; within just a few days I saw my job in a completely different light. I got up each morning alert and full of ideas as to how I would teach and implement that day's lessons. I brainstormed solutions to problems I was having with the people and the work I was doing. It was as though I was back in my first year of teaching, when I was enthusiastic and idealistic and nothing or no one could stop me. Throughout my day I reminded myself that a million dollar paycheck was awaiting me and that I would need to step up in a bigger ways if I wanted to be respected by my colleagues. It was intoxicating!

Evidently this new attitude was starting to pay off, as an administrator who had previously had little regard for me began to tell others what a fantastic job I was doing with the students. When she finally complimented me publicly at a staff meeting I almost fell off my chair.

Could it have been that I lost my joy for teaching because I had allowed it to become commonplace in my daily life?

This made me feel even more strongly about wanting to leave the school district and move on with my life in a direction that suited me in a way that would be fulfilling and rewarding, both personally and financially. I continued to better my best in everything I was doing in my life and it felt like I had been reborn.

You must find your own 'Why?' when it comes to transforming your life. Know that you will reinvent yourself many times in your life and that each transformation will bloom as a result of your wanting to do, be, and have more as a part of your life experience. Do not even try to do it all overnight, as your journey will be an important part of this joyous process and you don't want to miss a moment of it.

Make a list of the reasons why you are entertaining the idea of transformation at this point in your life. These may include a recent change in your circumstances, such as losing a loved one, going through a serious medical procedure, or having your finances be turned upside down after the loss of a job, a soured investment, or some other reason.

Whatever the case, approach each day knowing that you can transform yourself from where you are today into the person you have always wanted to be. My goal was to be able to replace my income with work I could do from home after having cancer multiple times, going through a serious work injury, and experiencing dissatisfaction with my work situation. That became my reason why and I moved forward in a way that would give me more of the life experience I was craving.

The bottom line is that consciously living with the intention of transforming your life and the way you do business either plays to your memories of a time where you were happy and successful or it plays to your hopes of having this type of life for the remainder of your time on earth.

Why You'll Want To Do Business With Transformational Entrepreneurs

In my way of understanding and belief it would just make sense that you would want to do business with people who are also more self-aware, conscious thinkers than the majority of the population. These people, it would seem, are the ones who change the world with their thoughts, ideas, and actions.

Make the decision to refuse to accept mediocrity and commonplace actions from this day forward and you will never go back to the way it was in the past.

This is almost an elitist way of thinking and behaving, in that you will be seeking out those people who have already shown they are living their lives with an elevated status. In this way we all become role models and mentors to each other, and those who continue to complain, refuse to take action, and seldom contribute to the joy, success, and well-being of those around them are slowly drummed out and replaced by small business owners and entrepreneurs who do make this effort on a consistent basis.

Resistance To Change

I used to always tell people that my first name, Connie, was Latin for 'constant, never changing', and that was why I did not like change one bit. If even the smallest detail of my daily existence changed abruptly then I was an unhappy camper.

The key to this is the word *abruptly*, as we all know that the world is in a constant state of flux, and that's why the law of homeostasis is so important in holding it all together. It turns out I was really only opposed to things changing right before my eyes, and not with the concept of intentional change over time.

The example I will share with you is that of my foray into the world of public speaking. For as long as I could remember I had a fear of speaking in front of adults. In the classroom for twenty years it was never an issue, but when I was in a room of any size made up of my peers I would freeze up and feel like I wanted to die. I'm being overly dramatic here, but you get the point. Even all those years ago I would have readily admitted this was due to my low self-esteem and lack of confidence in my own self worth and abilities.

Whenever this would come up people would advise me to join Toastmasters to learn how to speak in front of others. But I would vehemently protest that I did not want to speak to others in this way. The bottom line was that I did not believe that doors would open and opportunities would present themselves if I could speak publicly with some degree of effectiveness in sharing my message.

Fast forward to the fall of 2005, when I was just starting my new life as an entrepreneur and I began hearing how important it was to do some public speaking on your topic if you wanted to achieve any level of success and recognition in your field.

I could hear those little voices in my head, resisting abrupt change and intimidating me to the point where I just wanted to go home and hide under the covers. But this time was different, and I silenced the voices of doubt and allowed myself to be open to becoming a public speaker.

Within a few months I had joined the Rotary Club in Santa Clarita, California. Rotary is an international service organization with more than a million members worldwide that is involved in bringing clean water to third world countries and eradicating polio from our planet. Very quickly the microphone was being thrust at me so I could talk about our local projects, and within another few months my fear was dissipating.

Speaking first to the sixty members of my own Club, and then to several hundred Rotarians at the District level on the topics of social media and online marketing for small businesses made it possible for me to overcome my fear completely. I have now spoken to thousands of people around the world and enjoy it more than I ever thought possible. Loosen up on your resistance and you can move mountains.

Section III

What If You Transform?

"You can get everything in life that you want,
if you'll just help enough other people
to get what they want."
~Zig Ziglar

So, what if you make the decision to transform yourself and your business in this way? What can you likely expect as a result of your journey? Will it be worth the time and energy required to play full out and take your life experience to the next level *every single day*? Would it be worth it to do this every day for a year to be able to live the remainder of your life the way others only dream about?

These are the questions that you must answer for yourself so that your journey will be a satisfying one to you in regards to all aspects of your life. This is the quote I use regularly to describe what it means:

'Do for a year what others won't;
live the rest of your life the way others can't.'

In my own experience, I found that once I had made the decision to walk away from my previous life and start a new one I had an eerie feeling of calmness come over me. Even though I would never receive another paycheck from the school district or a commission or fee from my real estate work I knew that financially everything would work itself out. I thought of finances first because that had been a major struggle for me all of the years I had been in the work force. The fear of losing my home and of not being able to support myself and my elderly mother was a real one that I faced each morning when I woke up. I found it incredibly ironic that this feeling subsided once I had given up any chance of receiving income from teaching or real estate in the future.

Think about the reason you have stayed in a life situation that no longer serves you. Is it about the money and the security that brings? Or is it about the social connections that come about when you are spending your time each day with a select group of people? Our lives are interwoven with so many people and situations that you may have to dig deep to discover exactly what you need in order to feel fulfilled and that your life experience is a meaningful one. Connecting with and becoming a part of several charitable and service organizations was the catalyst that brought it all together for me.

Is It The Journey
Or The Destination?

When I began my path of discovering who I was and who I wanted to be back in 2005 I began to hear people quote Ralph Waldo Emerson, who said:

'Life is a journey, not a destination.'

The idea behind this quote, as interpreted by me and by people around the world since Emerson first said it during the 1800s, is that we are meant to enjoy every day for what it is and to feel as though we have never quite arrived at our destination. For as we move forward with our lives we continue to grow and change and evolve and the destination becomes more of a moving target.

I do not believe Emerson was correct in his statement of the human condition, or at least our interpretation of his statement. Instead, I feel that the quote should be this:

'The destination IS the journey.'

You read that correctly. My belief is that every single thing we think about, engage in, and pursue takes us to the exact destination we were seeking in the first place. You must choose this destination very carefully, take actions on what you wish to represent as a part of your life experience, and then enjoy every step of your journey as you move closer to the destination.

Now I realize this requires some mental gymnastics to get your head around this concept I am asking you to examine. Of course, the destination we choose even subconsciously at age eighteen will morph and evolve into something completely different and unrecognizable by age twenty-one, but the essence of who we are deep inside will not.

For example, I have loved animals since I was a toddler. This has manifested into a variety of formats and situations over the years, including my wanting to save all creatures in my own backyard, volunteering at the zoo while I was a teenager, majoring in biology during college so I could become a veterinarian, having a variety of domestic and exotic pets as an adult, donating to several animal rescues to help keep their doors open, writing about this to give further exposure, teaching my own children and now grandchildren about respecting and providing for animals, and having five dogs and a cat as my own pets right now.

Can you see the transgression of my original destination over a period of fifty years? My journey has consisted of many actions through the years that support and are congruent with my dream.

I could go on and on with other examples of how my destination has been my journey, including the story of how I came to be a classroom teacher.

Can you think of an example in your own life that supports this concept? It's both fascinating and eye-opening when you finally see how this all works and how our thoughts are things that guide us through our lives in a way that serves our belief system and values.

Lessons Learned
From The Classroom

During my twenty years as a classroom teacher I became keenly aware of the self-image my students had of themselves. They were only seeing themselves on that particular day, instead of being able to observe from the outside how far they had come from a point in the past. Allow me to explain further what I mean by this.

When a child is born the people around it are aware of every small detail pertaining to the new baby. During the first days and weeks every change is noteworthy, and is the topic of discussion with friends, family members, neighbors, and even complete strangers. Today the baby smiled, grasped a finger, followed movement with their eyes, and so on.

This process slows down to some degree as the baby gets older, and at this time it is only the people who are not directly involved in the daily life of the child who notice the small changes when they meet again. Comments like 'Look how much he's grown!' or 'Is she getting a new tooth?' draw attention to these subtle changes, but only for a moment when they are addressed in this way to the day to day caregivers for the child.

By the time that child is in school these notices tend to only come from family and friends who live far away and only see the child periodically. And at some point almost no one in the child's life would even comment on a change, other than to mention something about how they look or act today as opposed to some point in the distant past. Looking at old photographs sometimes becomes our only connection with the person we used to be.

It is no wonder that the children in my classrooms over the years were not aware, at least on a conscious level, of the fact that they were growing and changing and evolving every moment of every day. And until I began to think of life as an ongoing transformation I was yet another person in their life who did not see them as they really were - brilliant human beings who are constantly in the process of becoming the person they intend and want to be.

Right now I want you to look in the mirror and see who looks back at you. If you are my age you may see more gray hair or a wrinkle that was not there yesterday. If you are still in your twenties or thirties the changes may be much more subtle, such as a laugh line that is starting to form a crease near your mouth (known as a nasolabial fold)or hair that is not as thick as it once was.

The idea is to accept the fact that life is change and change is a choice, and that we can be in control of so much of this process throughout the remainder of our lives. I am not saying that we can eliminate the aging process completely, as that is a completely different conversation, but I am saying that we can move our lives forward in a direction of our choosing that will allow us to have a more satisfying and rewarding ride while we are alive here on earth.

What if we all become acutely aware of this idea of change and transformation as a natural part of life, knowing that we can be, do, and have anything we want in our lives? How would that change the way you live, learn, and take action with the things that have the most meaning for you?

Patience Can Be Overrated

Transformation can be a painful process, yet one that you will be grateful for as you make your journey. Whether you desire to transform yourself mentally, physically, spiritually, or in another way altogether, patience will be a virtue.

I first learned the value of patience while I was working as a classroom teacher. It would take months to receive new textbooks, to get the furniture we needed, and to arrange for a field trip, just to mention a few of the situations we encountered on a regular basis. Even though the other teachers and I knew exactly what needed to be done and how to do it, that did not necessarily translate to the administration being willing to help us make it happen.

One year we did not receive our mathematics books, workbooks, and manipulatives until right before the winter holidays. School had already been in session for four months by then, and the students had been expected to stay on the schedule set forth by the school district in terms of learning what they needed to know, so the teachers had become creative in figuring out how to best teach the concepts without the aid of books and material. We had looked through old books and items we already had, cleaned out our garages, and gone to yard sales to make sure our students had what they needed at their disposal. This worked very well, and everyone was progressing nicely. In fact, when the new books arrived none of us were particularly excited at the proposition of switching over to them. Instead, we did this slowly over the next month, replacing the old with the new in a deliberate way that made it almost fun. The idea of having the ultimate in patience skills continues to serve me to this day.

But the value of patience can be overrated, and I will go contrarian here and now warn you against becoming too patient when it comes to achieving your dreams and goals.

True entrepreneurs lose their patience very quickly as they wish to write and create at the speed of light.

I have seen too many people not take action and proclaim that they are not ready to make things happen, only to find that everything has changed when they finally take the time and make the effort to move forward. This has even happened to me a few times, making me even more aware of the pitfalls of having so much patience with yourself that you take no action at all.

Section IV

Beginning Your Transformation

*"The great dividing line between success
and failure can be expressed in five words;
"I did not have time".*
~Franklin Field

Wouldn't it be wonderful if we could just snap our fingers and change our lives dramatically for the better? Or how about going to sleep or taking a long nap and waking up with new and improved thoughts and ideas? I am reminded of a scene from the television situation comedy *All In The Family* with Archie and Edith Bunker, portrayed brilliantly by Carroll O'Connor and Jean Stapleton, where Edith is experiencing some of the side effects of menopause. Archie says this:

"If you're going to have a change of life you've got to do it right now. I'm going to give you just thirty seconds. Come on, now, change!"

This episode first aired in 1972 and has now become a classic on this topic. While we may chuckle as we think about it, the idea of spontaneous change is certainly an attractive one. If only it were that simple, especially if we have already been grateful for and appreciative of our journey so far. But alas, we must transform the old-fashioned way, earning our results one day and one action step at a time.

Accidental Transformation

Transformation sometimes occurs by accident, and I will share some examples of how this type of change has manifested in my own life.

The first time was when I got married at the age of sixteen to someone almost twelve years my senior. I went from being a footloose and fancy free junior high kid to being a wife, stepmother, and high school student (I was a freshman in high school during my first year of marriage). My husband had recently returned from serving in Viet Nam (another form of transformation I could never understand in full) and we spent much time during the early years of our marriage adjusting to life as a married couple. Looking back upon this time I realize that I took on a lot in terms of what would be expected of me, but it helped shape the person I was in the process of becoming. We had eleven years together until his life was cut short by leukemia. My stepchildren and I continue to be very close to this day, and they are now in their forties with children of their own.

Another time I was accidentally transformed was when I became a real estate appraiser in 1989. Prior to this I had worked as a real estate broker, listing and selling residential properties in the greater Los Angeles area.

One day a man came into the office I was working in and asked to see some of our files. I told him I needed to get permission from the manager before I could open up our filing cabinets for him to peruse. He nodded and sat down in a chair near the door.

I went to the back of the office to speak with the manager, who then told me these men came into the office regularly and that they just wanted to look at our information for their own purposes. They would then take this information and incorporate it into their reports and earn lots of money with them. These men were real estate appraisers.

I went back to the man and introduced myself. I told him he could look at anything we had if I could watch and ask a few questions. I promised not to get in the way and be a pest. He agreed; he returned once a week over the next couple of months, and three months later I was ready to take the state exam to become a certified residential appraiser. It was like magic!

By the first of the following year I was appraising after school and on weekends (I was still teaching in the classroom full time) and was earning so much money I didn't have time to pay off my bills quickly enough. I would sit down once a week and write checks to everyone I owed, and within about three months I had paid off my car in full and eliminated more than thirty thousand dollars of credit card debt.

The third time I accidentally transformed my life was when I woke up one day in April of 2005 and realized I was not living the life God had intended for me. It was both a sad day and an exhilarating one as I came to this realization. Even though I think of this as an 'accidental' occurrence at that point in time, what followed was most definitely on purpose and has continued to help me grow and mature as a human being.

Dealing With Difficult People

While I was a classroom teacher I was constantly pulled in several different directions with my thoughts, behavior, and actions. I was surrounded by many 'difficult' people, meaning they were people who did not enjoy working in a school setting, verbalized regularly about how much they disliked children, and were basically unhappy with their daily lives.

I knew this because they went on and on about how they should have chosen another career and why they just wanted to run away from their current home life. This shocked me. I had gone back to school to become a teacher at the age of thirty, and loved the idea of being with children all day in a caring, learning environment.

Some of the teachers screamed at their students regularly. I was appalled at this behavior and often said so to their faces. The administrators did not support the teachers with our ongoing struggles around teaching to the state tests, the curriculum, and the policies and it seemed that everyone was on edge.

Before I continue I will say that I am only speaking from my own personal experiences, and that I know for a fact there are many schools throughout the United States where things are handled much differently than what I was exposed to during my twenty years teaching in the Los Angeles area public schools.

One of my administrators, a principal, was particularly harsh and abrasive to me and to many other teachers for the six years I taught at that school. On an almost daily basis I found myself exhausted, stressed, and overwhelmed as a result of her unreasonable demands. Back then I blamed myself for not doing a good job, thereby accepting her accusations that I did not care about the children and was a terrible teacher.

My evenings and weekends were filled with guilt, because that was when I was working in real estate to be able to pay my bills and meet my other financial obligations. Even though there was no more I could be doing at night, on the weekends, and during holidays and vacations, the principal's words rang loudly in my ears nonetheless.

If you are dealing with difficult people in your life right now I would encourage you to do two things. First, devise a workable plan to get away from the person or people in question as soon as possible and second, begin the process of reframing their words and behavior so that your inner psyche isn't damaged any further.

Also, understand that if you continue to 'drive someone crazy' to the point where they seem to always be getting in your face and causing you unhappiness and pain, take responsibility for that and see how you can change your thinking and behavior to alleviate some of what is happening. This is part of what I recommend in terms of accepting responsibility for everything that occurs in your life. Never allow yourself to take on the 'victim' mentality.

In my case, it was the summer of 2004 that I began mentally outlining a two year escape plan. At the time I had no clue as to how I would ever be able to leave my teaching job without going into financial ruin, but I did not worry about that. Instead, I focused on the bigger picture of the life I wanted to create for myself.

Then I began to reframe the principal's outbursts in a way that worked for me. I imagined that she was screaming at me about every little issue because she knew that I was the most gifted classroom teacher on her staff. I envisioned her wanting me to change how I taught so that I could reach my true and full potential. Remember that I was deathly afraid of this woman and shuddered when she approached me, so this was most definitely a stretch of my imagination.

When I practiced this type of reframing for several weeks it began to make sense and take root in my subconscious. It was quite interesting to see how this manifested, and when she finally bragged to a small group of teachers how well I was teaching, no one, including me could believe their ears.

During these years I also developed the ability to compartmentalize my feelings when it came to this particular situation. I am not trained in psychology, but I have learned that the concept of compartmentalization is an unconscious psychological defense mechanism.

People use it as a means to avoid something called cognitive dissonance. This is the anxiety and mental discomfort caused by conflicting values and emotions. We are able to allow these conflicting ideas to live in our minds by acknowledging them within separate compartmentalized areas of our mind.

Simply stated, this psychological phenomenon allows each of us to separate out our feelings on different situations without losing our minds in the process. It is the mind's way of protecting itself during times of grief or sadness or other deep emotions.

Now I can look back on that entire six year ordeal with different eyes and feel like she did me a huge favor by being so hard on me every day. Not only did I learn to deal with and handle difficult people and situations, I also became a much stronger person who was preparing for life as an entrepreneur. I certainly would not have been in a position and frame of mind to help myself and others transform their lives if I had not gone though this experience in my own life.

I would encourage you to take similar actions if you are surrounded by even one difficult person. If not, you are allowing them to live rent free in your mind for as long as you tolerate their behavior and actions. As a transformation entrepreneur you have the choice to spend time only with the people who make your heart sing.

Transforming When You're Attracting The Wrong People Into Your Life

Years ago I chose to accept full responsibility for everything that occurs in my life. I mentioned this briefly in the previous sub-section of this book, on the topic of dealing with difficult people. This was not an easy choice, as there are many events which occur that even the most rational and logical person would agree that I was not to blame, such as the times I have gone through cancer treatment, the loss of a grandchild, Hurricane Andrew, or the Northridge earthquake. Yet I decided that if I took responsibility in this way I would never put myself in the position of making such a judgment call and would be able to more easily move forward in my life.

In August of 2014 my dear friend, business partner, and co-author Geoff Hoff came down with pneumonia and had to be hospitalized. He also has a history of heart disease, so this was quite serious. This happened late on a Thursday evening, and when our mutual friend Adrienne Dupree contacted me early the next morning I dropped everything to be at his side.

Geoff lives in Los Angeles, and the hospital he had been admitted to was located more than forty miles from me. I decided to take the Metrolink, southern California's commuter rail system to Union Station in downtown Los Angeles, and to then take the subway train to the station closest to the hospital. After that I would only be four blocks away from my destination.

Public transportation is not something that has been a part of my life over the years, except for the two years I lived in New York in my twenties, so perhaps I see it quite differently than someone who takes advantage of the convenience and cost savings on a regular basis. Nonetheless, after checking the schedule I ventured out to my local train station to purchase my ticket and then enthusiastically jumped aboard.

Two minutes after I disembarked I found myself in an unsavory section of downtown Los Angeles near the Staples Center. This is the multi-purpose arena where the Los Angeles Lakers and Clippers play basketball, as well as a venue for a great many musical, sporting, and other events throughout the year. For example, when Michael Jackson died in 2009 the family held a public service here, allowing almost twenty thousand fans to be a part of honoring their idol.

Anyway, when I looked around to get my bearings I saw that I needed to walk four more blocks in order to get to the hospital. I began walking and almost immediately was aware of someone coming up behind me at a rapid pace. This person ran at me full speed, knocking me to the ground in an instant. Everything went into slow motion as I fell to the ground, first hitting my head and arms on the pavement, then my feet and legs, and finally watching my purse came down beside me with a huge thud.

As I lay motionless in the street for what seemed like several minutes, I was aware of two men screaming and cursing. Soon I realized that the man who had assaulted me was being scared off by a second man. What was happening?

During this time I was not afraid for my life, and I didn't even think about being robbed. My fear was around my physical health, and being able to get to my feet and walk away from this incident. What if I had broken or sprained something and would not be able to get to my feet to walk away? What if my phone had broken and I wouldn't be able to call for help? These were my thoughts at that moment.

I then became aware of the second man standing over me. I reached out my hand, thinking he was going to help me to my feet. Instead, he began screaming at me to 'Get up!' and so I did, albeit very slowly.

Luckily, this story has a happy ending. As I got to my feet the people around me began to scatter, and I found myself standing all alone in the street. Quickly I took inventory of my situation; I was moving on my own steam and had not been robbed or physically assaulted.

I looked up at the skyscrapers forming the downtown skyline, spotted the street name I was looking for, and proceeded to hobble the four blocks to the hospital. I knew I was bleeding and scraped up pretty badly, but I waited until I was safely inside of the hospital to go into the restroom and have a closer look.

I mentioned that I now take full responsibility for everything that happens in my life, and this experience was no exception. If we are to experience life to the fullest we must expect things to not always turn out as we had planned. It is my belief that I attracted this crazy situation into my life and that I became stronger and more fully aware as a result.

Note: The following day a friend gave me a ride to and from the hospital because she coincidentally had a meeting less than a mile away. After that I drove my own car to the hospital each day I visited Geoff, which is an experience all its own in Los Angeles.

As for Geoff, he is doing well and making a full recovery and transformation of his own.

Writing Your Own Story

Every day we are given a blank slate and permission to start anew. We will encounter roadblocks and barriers, along with opportunities at every juncture. How we react and follow through with this gift of choice is completely up to us.

We must not dwell on what *was*; instead, get busy and do something! Throw away the old habits and templates and design the life you were meant to live.

Trust yourself and know that you have the abilities and the skills to accomplish all of your goals and dreams. This comes down to having the confidence to know that you can do, be, or have anything you want in your life.

Recently I mentored a private client who wanted to become a life coach to others in her church. She had gone back to school and received a master's degree in communication, and then went on to be certified as a life coach. Two years had passed without her taking any action with this, and few people outside her family and small circle of friends even knew she had completed this training.

When she came to me she lacked the confidence in her abilities to help others in this way, so we worked on a short presentation she could give to the women in her church group as part of an event they were having. In her presentation she addressed overcoming stress in your life, and in it she shared examples of how stress had manifested in her life over the years.

As I sat in the back of the room the night she presented to the group I realized that this was a powerful woman with so much to share. She was a natural in front of an audience, and even those who had not met her before felt comforted in her presence. She interacted with the group in such a way as is common of someone with years of speaking experience. I watched in awe as she controlled the room, speaking with both conviction and emotion about her topic.

The point I am making here is that we are all more powerful than we know or believe, and that you must write your own story and then be willing to share it with the world.

What's your story? I have used storytelling in my business since 2006, and this is how I have been able to come to terms with who I am and what I have to share. I love attending a live event and overhearing people describe who I am to others who are not familiar with me. They introduce me through my story, and each time I hear it I understand more about myself.

Pamela Slim discusses what she calls your 'Body of Work', and this includes your values, your beliefs, the problems you wish to solve, and the people you desire to serve. She says that when you harness your unique talents and beliefs that is the key to unleashing the power to be able to create the change we want to see in the world. Digging down and finding your roots helps you to reach into your own story and making yourself indispensable to the world. Your Body of Work builds your legacy and brings you security.

Take the time to write down and craft your story, ask others what they perceive to be your story, and then work on getting the story you are comfortable with out to the world. This one step, more than anything else you will ever do, will help you to achieve your goals and impact the people who will most benefit from hearing your message.

Consistent Actions Over Time

I steadfastly believe that we are all ordinary people capable of extraordinary actions and results. With this as a premise, isn't it possible that you are sitting on a wealth of information and ideas that could help transform your own life and the lives of others?

The Hopi Indians are a small group of Native American Indians living in northeastern Arizona in the United States. They use the word *Koyaanisqatsi* to indicate and describe a state of 'life out of balance' and the word *Powaqqatsi* meaning 'life in transition'. I often think of these two opposing concepts when thinking and writing about the process of transformation. If you are willing to take consistent action over time you can easily move from being out of balance to being in transition.

I did this when I came online in late 2005. I realized very quickly that I would need to write if I were to achieve even modest success as an online entrepreneur. The problem was that I had never done much writing, even though I had talked about it all of my life, all the way back to my childhood. I made the conscious decision to write one article every day for one hundred days during the spring of 2007. This self-imposed challenge ended up only taking me not one hundred days to complete, but only seventy-eight days, and during that time I had established myself and taken up the habit of daily writing.

Nine years later, as I pen this tenth book, I can attest to the validity of this concept of taking consistent action over time. You can do this in any area of your life and experience your own extraordinary results. Every day, in every way you're closing in on your life's dreams and goals. Choose to move from being out of balance to living a life in transition and transformation. It will be worth it, I promise you.

Massive Productivity and Time Management

A television talk show host named Art Linkletter had an afternoon show during the 1960s I used to watch after school each day with my mother. One of the segments involved Art going into the studio audience and selecting someone at random to speak with. They would converse for a few minutes and then set the clock for sixty seconds and continue talking. If the person could tell Art when the minute was up, give or take ten seconds, they would win a prize. It was very rare when someone was able to do this because time is such an elusive entity in our mind.

I never even thought about being productive and managing my time during the first fifty years of my life, yet now I am considered to be an expert in this area. How could this be? Is it possible to have a gift and talent for something that doesn't manifest itself until you are quite a bit older? I will share what I have learned about productivity, accountability, time management and more as an entrepreneur in a way that will allow you to explore these areas in your life and learn about small changes you can make that will bring you huge results.

Being productive and achieving your goals and dreams in record time is not a skill you are born with. As Brian Tracy has said, 'All skills in business are *learnable* skills.' I strongly believe that you must nurture these traits in order to maximize them. By doing so you reprogram your brain in a way that makes permanent alterations to the way you think, act, and follow through with the tasks you are regularly confronted with in your daily life. It is my intention with this work to help take you from where you are today to closer to where you want to be in your personal life, your business, and with anything that is of importance to you.

I am often asked if I'm productive all of the time or if it just seems that way. The simple answer to this is that I am always productive, unless I am not feeling well or on an extended vacation. Once I embraced this way of living, everything changed in both my personal and professional life. Organization, focus, clarity, and time management are all a part of this for me. Massive productivity has allowed me to accomplish much more in my life than I ever thought possible.

Let's get started by looking at some examples of how maximizing your productivity in your business can increase your bottom line. This exercise alone will help you to transform your thinking and actions in a way that will serve you well.

My background is similar to that of many entrepreneurs I know today. I started out working at various jobs after graduating from college in 1977. These included managing a coin laundry, working at the phone company as a shift supervisor, being an outside sales representative for a telecommunications company, selling cars, working as a claims adjuster for a nationally known insurance company, and assisting a veterinarian with surgeries on small animals.

Each job started out as one of interest to me, only to find out that it would not hold my interest for the long term. This was during my twenties and led to frustration, low self-esteem, confusion, and an overall sense that I would not fit in anywhere. Where was my place in the working world?

In 1983 I decided to go for my real estate license, in hopes that this career would be a satisfying one for me. I signed up for a six week class to learn some basics about residential and commercial real estate, prepared for the exam, and promptly failed it on my first try. There were a hundred and fifty multiple choice questions and you needed to answer at least one hundred and five of them correctly in order to receive a passing score of seventy percent. My score was a ninety-nine, six questions short of hitting the mark.

I remember feeling like a complete failure after learning that I had not passed the state exam. It was also quite embarrassing for me, because I was used to scoring very well on tests while I was in school. I had read and reviewed all of the materials and came to the conclusion that I just wasn't smart enough to do this and did not have an aptitude for this career in real estate.

Several days later I was discussing what had happened with a close friend. I'll never forget what he said to me that day.

"Take the test again. I'll bet lots of people don't pass it the first time, just like lots of other tests."

He went on to give examples of how many attorneys do not pass the Bar exam on the first, or even the second attempt. He also mentioned people he knew personally who had failed exams initially and then gone on to successful careers in their chosen field. Some people even fail their driver's license exam the first time, but they generally always go back for a second try, many times only twenty-four hours later.

Now I really felt stupid. Had it not occurred to me that I could retake this real estate exam? I had heard that you had to wait six weeks to take it again after failing and now almost a week of precious time had already passed. I hurriedly signed up so that I would have my spot reserved to take it again. Then I returned to the real estate school and told them I wanted to study more to learn what I needed to pass the exam. They were caring and helpful as they provided me with more practice exams and resource materials to read and spend time with at home.

During the next few weeks I was completely focused on learning. Looking back, I think this was perhaps this was my first foray into the world of productivity, as I began organizing my notes, thoughts, and ideas about real estate and the information I would need to pass the test and keep on moving into this new career. I was excited at the possibilities of helping others to buy and sell property and to find good opportunities for myself at the same time. I allotted time each day, seven days a week to learning, studying, and reviewing the concepts I was expected to know.

When my big day arrived a month later I drove into downtown Los Angeles with an air of confidence I had seldom felt in my lifetime up to that point. As I was sitting in the exam room taking the test I knew that I would pass this time because I was better prepared and had a different mindset than I had had six weeks earlier.

Ten days later my envelope arrived with my exam results. I had passed! They do not give you your score when you pass, but I'm sure it had to be ninety percent or more. I was elated and knew that I had achieved my goal and would now be able to move forward with my dream of a career in real estate.

I was twenty-eight years old at the time, and knew so little about productivity and time management. In my mind and way of thinking it was only important that I had passed the exam, not that I could use these same exact principles and strategies to assist me every day for the rest of my life. I would not learn that until more than twenty years later.

I muddled through the rest of my twenties and into my thirties, never taking enough time or making a big enough effort to climb out of mediocrity. I was enjoying the idea of working in real estate and even went on to become a Broker instead of remaining as an agent. But I still did not earn enough money from this to support myself. Jobs became boring to me and I continued to find myself in various positions.

Fast forward to the new millennium and here is what occurred...

In 2012 I decided to write yet another book, this time on the topic of time management for entrepreneurs. I called Geoff Hoff and asked him to co-author it with me. When I told him I wanted to write a twenty thousand word book in seven days there was a short pause on the other end of the line before he answered with an enthusiastic 'Yes!'

We actually completed this book, *Time Management Strategies for Entrepreneurs: How to Manage Your Time to Increase Your Bottom Line* in about five days and used the remainder of the time to design a cover and start marketing it online.

We can't talk about productivity without a discussion of time management. I never thought of myself as someone who managed my time well, but since becoming an online entrepreneur that has been one of the areas I am known best for within my circle of influence. We all have twenty-four hours each day, but understanding how to effectively delegate each of those hours is another story.

I utilize the concept of something I refer to as 'Prime Time' to maximize my efficiency each and every day. It is taken from what the television networks have always called the hours between eight and eleven in the evening. Your prime time is the best time of day for you to have clarity, focus, and the ability to accomplish your tasks quickly and easily.

My own prime time is in the early morning, specifically between six and eleven every day. I make an effort to work for at least three of those hours, three days a week to write, think, and create for my business.

Delegation is the best thing since sliced bread and I'll address this topic again later on in the book. I used to try to do everything myself, and that soon wears you out and makes you feel like a failure. It was a sixth grade student named Claire who first convinced me of the importance of delegating tasks to others that they could better accomplish.

One day after school I was cleaning the windows, sweeping, and just doing an overall cleanup in my classroom. Claire and a few other girls walked by the room and saw me hard at work. It was Claire that said to me,

"Mrs. Green, why don't you let us help you with this work? We have to clean at home, but at school it's fun. We could also probably do it better than you, if you don't mind me saying this. Then you'd have more time to grade papers and do the work only teachers can do."

So there it was. Claire had voiced what no one else had ever said to me before. I handed her the broom, stepped aside, and went back to my desk. She had changed my life forever, even though neither of us knew it at the time.

Are there areas of your life where you can put these techniques into action right away?

Pomodoro Technique

I also use a timer to make sure I work in uninterrupted blocks of time each morning. This is based on something called the Pomodoro Technique, developed by Francesco Cirillo. You can read more about this and why it is so effective at the link I've added to the Resources section at the end of the book.

I have small dogs, so I take a break after thirty or forty-five minutes of working and spend time playing with them. We all go outside for ten to fifteen minutes and the fresh air and joy of being with them rejuvenates me to be able to work for an additional block of time. I have been able to write nine books using this technique, as well as create more than thirty information products, many presentations, and even more for my online business. It will work in any niche and for anything you wish to accomplish in your life.

Staying focused on your project from start to finish is an important one for every entrepreneur. Many of us tend to be swayed by the latest and greatest product, course, or idea that shows up, abandoning our original idea in favor of a new one. These are referred to as BSOs (bright, shiny objects) and I challenge you to not get caught up with something new unless your current project becomes unviable for a specific reason or for an extended period of time.

Instead, step away from what you're working on and come back to it twenty-four hours later with fresh eyes and an improved outlook and attitude. This will enable you to see your project from a different perspective and to add to it in a way you previously may not have thought about.

We all have the same twenty-four hours each day. It's completely up to you to utilize them in a way that will serve you well.

Helping Others To Transform

It has always been my intention, for as far back as I can remember, to help other people make changes to their lives that will give them a more rewarding overall life experience. This can be done on a conscious level through mentoring, and on a deeper, almost subconscious level by just becoming a good listener and being willing to share what you know and believe with those who are interested.

In July of 2014 my extended family came to the United States for the very first time for a month long visit. It was a trip of a lifetime, and we were able to do all of the things we had talked about doing during the previous several years while I was visiting them in Europe.

I had been spending a month every summer visiting them over in Finland, but it is a much simpler task for one person to go abroad than for two adults and four children to do it in the opposite direction.

My goal and intention for their visit was to give them the opportunity to experience everything they had ever heard about in America. That included Disneyland, Santa Barbara, going to the beach, the water parks, shopping, and so much more. The planning and logistics took about six months to organize, and it was quite expensive as well.

I wanted all of them to know that I was prepared to help them do anything they might want to be a part of in the United States, then or in the future. This would include an exchange program for my eldest granddaughter, business connections for my stepdaughter and son-in-law, and a host of other things that could enhance their lives in the years to come. They are so special to my life and have done so much for me over the years that I wanted to reciprocate in any way possible.

The vacation was a wonderful one for all of us and I was sad to see them go back to Finland.

They were not home more than three days when I received an email from my stepdaughter. In it she shared that I had inspired her during our visit and made her feel like she honestly could achieve any goals she set for herself. She had decided to return to school to earn her degree in nursing, and had enrolled in school that would begin in two weeks.

I was overjoyed at this news! Helping someone to transform their life and reach for their dreams is a worthwhile goal.

Transformation And Entrepreneurial Success

You must choose to make a commitment to your own life transformation. As Pat Riley, then head coach of the Los

Angeles Lakers basketball team said, 'You're either in or you're out. There is no in between.'

Author Richard Koch, best known for *The 80/20 Principle: The Secret to Achieving More with Less* teaches a concept of working one hour each day to get off of the 'hamster wheel' for good. I can personally attest to the power of doing this, as when I came online and made the decision to write for an hour each day. This single action, which turned into a habit after a few weeks transformed me from someone who had always wanted to write into a bestselling, published author who now writes every single day.

As a transformational entrepreneur you will understand that it takes a village of people and a holistic approach to help yourself and everyone you are associated with to reach their true and full potential.

Hopefully by now you are beginning to understand the importance of transformation, and how entrepreneurs and small business owners can facilitate a change in the world through their interactions with their own customers and clients. The impact of our day to day lives has such far reaching consequences that are almost impossible to project. Offer your products and services with kindness, integrity, and the true spirit of serving and watch as your business grows and expands.

Section V

Entrepreneurial Transformation: A Blueprint

'We must be willing to let go of the life we had planned, so as to have the life that is waiting for us.'
~E. M. Forster

I have always maintained that entrepreneurs do not need or even want a blueprint for success. If you'd like for someone to tell you exactly what to do and when to do it, get a job and the supervisor or boss will be glad to dictate how you spend your time each day. This includes when you will arrive and leave each day, when and where you will eat, and when you will be allowed to use the restroom facilities. Many jobs even have rules about what types of behavior and activities you may engage in when you are off the clock, and how long you must wait before starting your own business of a simple nature.

On the opposite end of the spectrum are entrepreneurs, described as creative risk takers who make decisions on the fly based on what works for them and where they want to venture next. Part of the allure of having your own business is this very idea of having total and complete control to create your own blueprint for life, of which your business is a huge part.

However, with this said I will tell you that I had to develop a blueprint for myself when I began back in 2006 or I would most likely have never achieved enough success to make it all worthwhile, financially or otherwise. I am more than happy to share this outline for success with you here. Breaking it all down into steps will make it even more clear, I believe.

The Ten Magic Steps

I have identified ten steps that will get you into the frame of mind and psychological mindset of a transformational entrepreneur.

Believe that you can have, do, and be whatever you want, and achieve anything you want as a part of your life experience. Young children get this, but as we enter school and have more and more experiences outside the realm of close family we tend to forget and lose faith in this concept. Suspend reality just long enough to understand and believe that you have the tools, resources, and support to do just about anything you can imagine.

Decide exactly what it is you do want. Most people never find satisfaction because they were never clear about what they wanted to begin with. What do you want your life and business to look like? Remember that entrepreneurs *choose* the type of business they run, how and when they run it, and the people they want to be involved with on a daily basis. Choose well and you will never work another day for the rest of your life.

Choose a Mentor in several areas of your life. Mentors are individuals who take you under their wing and help you to develop a pathway to your goals in specific areas. I was not even familiar with the concept of having a mentor until 2005. That was when I met Raymond Aaron at a real estate conference in Los Angeles. He was speaking on the topic of 'living a mentored life' and suddenly it became clear to me that I was attempting to go through my life all on my own, without seeking and benefitting from the wisdom of someone who had gone before me.

Raymond soon became my first official mentor, even though I learned that we are informally mentored by others from the time we can walk and talk. I have gone on to have many mentors for my business over these past nine years, and now know exactly what I need and what best suits me when it comes to choosing someone to work with in this way.

Learn how to do what you want to do. When I made the conscious decision to become an online entrepreneur I had to learn many new skills, including some specialized writing, computer technology, and networking with others who were already successful in this area. Immediately I began taking online courses, reading books, and reaching out to others who could answer my questions and help me move forward more quickly.

Be willing to do the work. The first few months were rough for me because I didn't have a schedule or a plan of how I was going to move forward. I realized very quickly that this would be hard work, so I buckled down and made it happen. This required much more discipline on my part than I was used to.

As an employee for the school district I knew what they expected me to do each day. The only discipline required was to show up on time, be prepared, and complete the work assigned to me. As a small business owner in real estate a little more was required in that I had to seek out the job assignments, complete them adequately, and then move on to the next assignment.

As an online entrepreneur I was one hundred percent responsible for making my business happen! This was a huge realization when I saw that if I took little or no action then I did not earn any income that day. It only took a few weeks before I figured out that I had to spend time each day with income generating activities before I could do anything else. It didn't take long before I got into the rhythm of what my work day would look like and I was then able to expand into areas that would build my business for the long term, instead of just going through the tasks required to meet my most immediate financial needs.

Don't let the details get in your way - don't sweat the small stuff. As you embark on a new endeavor there are so many things that will get in the way. These can be stumbling blocks or opportunities to grow and expand your thinking and knowledge base. For me, the details of technology were making me feel like I could not achieve my goals, so I outsourced ninety-nine percent of that and only learned what I needed to do on a daily basis. The results have been phenomenal as my progress skyrocketed once I no longer had to think about what I didn't know and did not want to learn.

Believe in magic and expect miracles. Look to the children in your life for this one. While my family was visiting from Finland we spent time at Disneyland. It seems that Mickey Mouse is universally loved and they wanted to see Mickey's house in the 'Toon Town' section of Disneyland.

I will share the shortened version of this story here. After waiting in line for twenty minutes or so, the adults in our group were ready to get out of line and move on to other attractions. The children, however, ranging in age from five to fourteen, were quite satisfied to wait for as long as it took to get to the end of the line and experience the magic they believed would be there.

Almost two hours later we did finally make it to the end, and spending time alone with Mickey Mouse and my family was most definitely worth. To think that we could have missed this because of the impatience on the part of the grownups is beyond my imagination. The young ones reminded us all that day what it means to believe in magic and expect miracles.

Pay it forward forever. There will be people in your life that will step up and help you when no one else will. Remember who they are and be prepared to reciprocate forever. When I think back to my humble beginnings, it was people like Jeanette Cates and Joe Vitale who gave me a hand up. My students are also very special to me and I look for every opportunity to help them shine and show them off in a special light.

Start from where you are. You don't want or need to transform over night, and in fact, this will be an ongoing process for the remainder of your life. We are all at different points along the continuum, and occasionally we meet up at a common point. Then that time passes and again we are moving along on our journey. Enjoy wherever you happen to be and know that if you have made the commitment to succeeding then everything will unfold with grace and ease.

Get started today! There is no reason not to go for your dreams and goals right this second. If not you, who? If not now, when? Do not hesitate even one more day to get started or continue on the road to achieving your goals and dreams.

Masterminds with Like-Minded People

Man is not an island. I can remember hearing that when I was very young and not being exactly sure of what it meant. Over time I came to understand that people must be exposed to other people in order to move forward, achieve goals, and enjoy a satisfying and fulfilled life. As a young adult in the work force I was constantly frustrated by the people I was with on a daily basis. This led to my becoming extremely judgmental and resentful around people with whom I did not see 'eye to eye'.

I would sit through our meetings with something of a scowl on my face, the inner turmoil eating me up inside. Then I would go home and complain to anyone who would listen about how awful it was to have to work with people who just didn't 'get it'.

Those days are long over now that I'm an online entrepreneur. Because I work for myself and make all of the decisions as to how, when, where, and with whom I work, I am able to connect with the exact people I wish to spend time with by putting together something called a Mastermind. In fact, I am currently a member or a leader of several Mastermind groups.

Masterminds have been around for centuries, and Napoleon Hill brought them to the mainstream in his book *Think and Grow Rich*. One of my favorite sections of this book is his chapter on The Driving Force: The Ninth Step Toward Riches. Hill defines a Master Mind as a 'Coordination of knowledge and effort, in a spirit of harmony, between two or more people, for the attainment of a definite purpose.' He then goes on to explain how, with a carefully selected group of people, you'll most definitely be able to achieve all of your goals and objectives quite easily and without duress.

Napoleon Hill further breaks down this process into two distinct parts, one part which is economic and the other one spiritual. The economic portion may seem obvious, as by surrounding yourself with people who can give you specific and excellent advice, ideas, and support when it comes to your business that will most definitely lead to its financial success.

On the other hand, the spiritual portion is more intangible. When two or more people come together for the purpose of discussing, planning, and 'thinking out loud' about the thoughts and ideas they have been entertaining, a third entity is created that is almost like have another member of the group.

I have been running Masterminds as a part of the Retreat I host several times each year in Santa Barbara since 2011 and can tell you that what all of us have been able to achieve in nothing short of miraculous. There is something about moving out of your comfort zone that gives you permission to think and speak more freely than you have in years. Most people do not live at the beach, so the salty sea air works like a business aphrodisiac to help open up the lines of communication between your inner and outer consciousness. I love watching people 'let go' of the day to day rigors and confines we have all experienced at one time or another.

Transforming Your Income With Multiple Streams

Over these past nine years I have learned so much about what it takes to become a successful entrepreneur. It's been an education unlike anything I've ever been through in my life, including attending law school for a year and a half, working on an MBA, and earning my teaching credential. It's been an incredible journey that I would not trade for anything.

I started out with affiliate marketing, as I had no products of my own and wanted to start earning money as quickly as possible. It's funny, when I think back, that my belief was that I would only recommend other people's products and services until I had enough of my own products. The fact is that almost half of my income continues to come from the products, services, and courses I recommend through affiliate links.

Remember that my goal for the first year and a half of working online was only to replace the income I had given up as a classroom teacher and real estate broker/appraiser. This amounted to approximately one hundred twenty-five to one hundred fifty thousand dollars a year, in United States currency. When I did achieve that goal at the end of 2007 I suddenly realized that I could go further in my life if I continued to earn more income and build an online empire.

That's exactly what I have done over the years, thus creating eight stream of income for myself, which include:

- Digital Information Products
- Local Business Marketing
- Niched Affiliate Sites
- Corporate Consulting
- Amazon Kindle/Authorship
- Coaching/Mentoring/Retreats
- Hosting Your Own Live Events
- Physical Products on Amazon

The idea of having multiple streams of income is not a new one. In fact, I understood this concept, at least to some degree when I chose to continue working in real estate after I earned my teaching credential and took a full time classroom assignment. Even back then I understood the importance of having two different sources of income. This was facilitated because of the teacher's strike that took place during my first year of teaching and stuck with me for all of my twenty years working at four different schools.

Working online opens the doors to a variety of global opportunities to serve others while also increasing our income. I recommend starting with just one or two of the income streams I outline above that resonate with you and then growing your business over time to where it feels right for you and your goals.

New Rules for Living
A Transformational Life

I believe that we must have order and balance in our lives before we can achieve any true success. This goes back to the Hopi Indians words *Koyaanisqatsi* to indicate a state of 'life out of balance' and the word *Powaqqatsi* meaning 'life in transition' I mentioned earlier. Most of us are experiencing Koyaanisqatsi in our lives, whether it is obvious to see or not. One small misstep and our world begins to fall apart. The goal is to move closer to Powaqqatsi, where transitioning from one experience to another is a comfortable and successful part of your daily life.

- *Family/Friends* - These are the people you hold dear and choose to spend your precious time with. It doesn't matter if they are blood relatives, extended family, or wonderful neighbors; they are the human beings who you need in your daily life and whom also need you in theirs and will make your heart sing, no matter what the circumstances. If I am being totally honest I will tell you that I did a terrible job of cultivating and maintaining these types of relationships until I began my transformation in 2005. Now I go out of my way each day to connect with someone and let them know just how special they are in my life.
- *Faith* - If you understand that you will always receive what you believe, then you have faith in your heart. This has nothing to do with organized religion and doctrine, unless that is what feeds your soul. Faith goes much deeper and connects you with your source and maker. Carefully guard where you choose to place your faith, as it does make a difference in your outcomes.

- *Health* – Believe it or not, the state of your overall health will have a direct correlation as to how productive and successful your life can be. I have recently begin the practice of fasting for at least twelve hours one day a week and love how this has enhanced my thought process. Take complete responsibility for what you eat and drink and how you move your body for optimal health every day.

- *Focus/Foundations* - Your Core Values allow you to build a foundation for your life on your terms. This requires you to make a conscious decision as to what you want your life to look like. Many people simply inherit their values and beliefs from their family and friends and don't take the time to explore other options. Make yours a choice. Don't just know what you believe, know why you believe it. What you focus on expands. Take full and total responsibility for what goes on inside your head, within your daily actions and behavior, and how you interact with those around you.

- *Finances* - Know your numbers! I continue to be amazed at how many entrepreneurs, even those who have achieved some level of success, have no clue where they income is coming from each month or how they can increase it the following month. A business of any kind is considered to be a 'going concern' if it can meet all of its financial obligations and has enough resources to continue to operate indefinitely and without a loss. If you are using credit cards and commingling personal funds then you must get a handle on this situation immediately if you are to transform your life and your business.

- *Fun* - Life will be much more enjoyable if you get everything else in your life organized and on track. Schedule the fun activities that give you pure joy and work hard so that you will feel like you deserve to have fun on a regular basis. At this point in my life I spend an equal number of hours each week on work and fun. And if you truly love what you do you'll never work another day in your life. It took me over two years of working diligently to get to this point, but now I can live the remainder of my life knowing that I have this balance.

These six core concepts are the basis of my life and make it possible for me to now live every day on my terms. I feel like I am deserving of the best life possible, and that I can only help others if I have helped myself first. It's like what they tell you when you fly in an airplane; affix your own oxygen mask first before attempting to help anyone else, including young children or the elderly.

Rules/Strategies for a Revolutionary Transformation:

- Clarity and focus as to what you really want to achieve
- Commitment of your time, resources, ideas
- Mentorship in all areas of your life
- Responsibility for what occurs
- Determination to succeed in what you set forth to conquer
- Perseverance to finish what you start
- Enlightenment to go further in your thinking

Let's take a closer look at each of these.

Clarity and focus as to what you truly want to achieve is crucial in all areas of our life. We all tend to be much too vague when it comes to this, so I will share how I have been able to maintain clarity and focus in my own life.

For each action, or inaction I take each day I ask myself if this is bringing me closer to my goals or further away. For example, if my goal is to lose weight and become more fit and healthy then I would ask myself if sitting at the computer for the first hour of my day is serving me in regards to this specific goal.

Now this brings up a great point, in that you may have overlapping goals that require you to choose which one you will focus on at a time. I write first thing in the morning, so I made the conscious decision to go to bed an hour earlier each night so that I'd be more alert and fresh early in the morning to write for an hour or so. Then I go out for my walk, so I'm able to accomplish both goals within a couple of hours each day.

Transformation takes deep desire, time, mentorship, and the willingness to show up and do the work.

Commitment of your time, resources, and ideas goes back to what I said earlier. If you are merely interested in something you will do what is convenient in order to achieve it. If you are honestly committed, you will do whatever it takes to achieve your goals and more. Write down exactly what it is that you are willing to commit to for the next thirty days, and then take it from there.

Mentorship in all areas of your life means that you never have to walk alone. Look around and see if you currently have a friend or relative you would consider to be a mentor to you. This is where the concept will begin, but choosing a mentor to learn from to achieve specific goals must come next. I currently pay half a dozen people to guide me in several areas of my life. These are typically paid relationships with boundaries that will help you go from where you are right now to closer to where you want to be.

Responsibility in all areas of your life. I love this quote from Les Brown on this topic:

"Accept responsibility for your life. Know that it is you who will get where you want to go, no one else."

I have to admit that I did not take full responsibility for everything that occurred in my life before coming online. Now that I do, more doors have opened and opportunities presented themselves in a way that I could never have previously imagined.

This concept may be a difficult one to get your head around, so start by taking responsibility for something so far removed from you that it almost seems ridiculous to do so. Examples of this would be to take responsibility for the weather or for the outcome of a political election. This will certainly make you think, if nothing else.

Determination to succeed in everything you set forth to conquer. Everything you choose to do is worth your greatest effort. Promise yourself you will do whatever it takes to succeed and not let anyone or anything get in your way. If someone tries to dissuade you or convince you that you cannot do something, politely excuse yourself from the conversation and keep moving forward.

Perseverance to finish what you start. I used to be a quitter. I would get very excited about something and then give up a short time later. When I think back to everything I missed over the years because of my lack of commitment to persevere it saddens me. Be willing to finish what you start every time and see how fast and how far you will go in your life.

Enlightenment is the yearning to go further with your thinking. We are ever-changing, growing, evolving, transformational beings. Once you accept that concept and idea into your subconscious you will long to learn more and enjoy the benefits of the enlightened life.

If You Don't Have An Assistant, You Are One!

The first time someone said this to me I was taken aback and did not respond out loud. A few minutes later it finally hit me that she was correct about this, and we proceeded to have a conversation about how I could make this change in my business and my life.

Working completely alone is all about power and control. Giving at least a little bit of this up in order to grow a bigger business may take some getting used to, but it will be worth it in the long run.

The very first thing I outsourced was technology tasks because I simple could not set up an online business using the limited skills I had acquired. Because I had no choice in this matter if I wanted to build a business based primarily on the Internet, it almost did not feel like outsourcing.

Next, I found someone to submit my articles to the directories and distribution sites. Although I continue to do all of my own writing and pride myself on this fact, getting that writing out to the world is not something I need to be involved in directly. Instead, I have people who syndicate my content through a variety of channels each week to increase my exposure and credibility.

Finding the right people to help you does not have to be an arduous task. Ask people already working in your field for their recommendations, meet people in person at live events, and visit the freelancing sites online to see who is available. Connecting with people who can become a part of your virtual team is crucial to your success and goals.

Spiritual Transformation

Making the decision to transform my life spiritually meant leaving people from my former life behind. I found I had less and less in common with them and that I was finding their beliefs and actions to be 'wrong' and not serving them at all by spending time with them. I came to accept that I create my own reality and my life experience with every action, choice, and thought I allow myself to participate in, and this included the people I chose to spend time with.

Part of spiritual transformation can begin with letting go of things from your past to make space for what is new. I'll share just one example of how this concept has served me over these past few years.

In 2009 I started something called the 30 Day Power Blogging Challenge. It was extremely popular and people from around the world joined me in the challenge. Those who were able to follow through and post to their blog for thirty days in a row got a mention in my emails and on my blog. I repeated it again over the next three years and its popularity grew immensely. The idea was that blogging was the stepping stone to creating great content for articles, short reports, information products, and books. Being the creator and also a participant in this Power Blogging Challenge each time put me in the unique position of being able to help others while also helping myself. We could all increase our credibility and visibility with our writing, and ultimately the profitability would follow. In 2012 I made the decision to let this Challenge go because I seemed to be the only one who had followed through from the initial blogging to the creation of products and books. If there was no direct benefit to my community then it simply did not make sense for me to continue.

A year later two online business coaches who had been a part of what I was doing decided to start their own challenge. When I first saw what they were doing I questioned whether they were copying me. Upon closer examination I saw that they were doing this for the same reasons that I had in the beginning. I wished them well and sat back to observe. It was an important part of my transformation process for me to 'let go' of what I had started in order to make room in my business for new and exciting things to take place. Instead of feeling hurt or angry I was willing to acknowledge that others can take over where you left off and everyone can move forward in a positive way.

The Writing Habit

The following is an excerpt from a white paper I prepared on the topic of writing to expand your business. I believe it is apropos for what you'll want to accomplish as a transformational entrepreneur.

"Are Writers Born Or Made?"

I now earn my living as an author and a speaker, but the path to this point in my life has not been a linear one. Instead, it has been one fraught with fear, inaction and self-doubt. Moving past these beliefs and on to ones of confidence in myself and a belief that writing is a way to serve others has brought me full circle to where I am today. As I think back over the years the question was always:

"Are writers born or made?"

It was during the fifth grade when I first experienced the writing bug. A boy in my class, Danny, was known for writing the most interesting stories and he asked me to help him write one for our winter program. Instantly I went from being just another fifth grader to being a person of great interest to the other kids, the teacher, and to my mother. It was then that I became keenly aware of the impact writing could have on others, and perhaps that was part of the allure for me.

During my two weeks of coming out of the shadows to help Danny write his story, I stepped up to the challenge in the best way I knew how at the time. I took this opportunity quite seriously. Sitting down at our dining room table I would pour over what he had written and think long and hard about what I could add to the story to continue along with his thoughts and ideas. As each day passed I became braver, adding a comma or a phrase here or there, but never, ever removing or changing what he had written.

It never occurred to me to alter Danny's original story idea in any way. Even at the tender age of ten I believed that my ideas were inferior to those of others. The voice in my head told me to help Danny to write *his* story, to not make any changes or even any suggestions for change, and to be grateful that he was allowing me into this sacred world of the writer. The story was finished and the school's winter program was a success, but my feelings of insecurity when it came to my own writing would stick with me for years to come. Danny had been born a great writer, and I had not.

During high school and college I again ventured down the road of desiring to write short stories, teleplays (stories written for episodic television) and even screenplays. However, my fears of rejection and self-doubt were so strong at this point in my life that I seldom started, yet alone finished any writing of my own. Even when I was taking a writing class I would wait until the very last moment to write something, which allowed for me to get credit for the class but never to grow from the experience or to improve my writing.

Many years later I would become a classroom teacher. The overwhelming majority of my students spoke English as a second language. English can be a difficult language to master, and it was the writing they struggled with most. I promised them this would greatly improve if they would commit to writing for one hour every single day. This was met with groans of displeasure, but those children who took my advice went on to academic achievement and personal satisfaction. None of them had been born a writer, but with daily practice many excellent writers were made in my classroom.

Looking back, I am not sure where I came up with the idea that writing every single day would make the writing better. Perhaps it was just common sense on my part and finally having the confidence to share what I believed to be true and helpful to others.

After twenty years in the classroom I left my former life behind and came online in hopes of becoming a successful entrepreneur. I realized almost immediately that writing would be an integral part of my journey. It was time for me to believe in myself, move past the fear, and to apply the advice I had given in the classroom to my own life.

Every day I wrote something; an article, a blog post, and email to my list. I even challenged myself to write one hundred articles in a hundred days and completed this task in only seventy-eight days! I celebrated each small victory and allowed my confidence to grow and my thinking to expand. During the past seven years I have written nine bestselling books and seldom go a day without writing. These days it is as though divine intervention is beside me as the words flow out of my mind and on to the page.

Some writers are born and others are made. Either way, getting your thoughts out of your head and onto the paper (or into a word processing document) will help you to transform joyously as you express your ideas, feelings, and beliefs over time. Examine your gifts and keep moving forward to see which will be true for you.

The Four Stages of Competence

True transformation can only take place from within. If you are inspired or encouraged by an outside force, such as a person, a book, or something else in your realm of consciousness to make a drastic change to your life you must do it for yourself and for no one else.

This model was first developed by psychologist Noel Burch in the 1970s when he was working at a company called Gordon Training International.

The first stage is that of unconscious incompetence, where you do not know what you do not know. You are like a newborn baby, experimenting with ways to get from the stage where you can finally roll over and hold up your head to the point where you can pull yourself up and begin to walk. Fortunately, we have adults supporting and encouraging our progress at this point in our development and transformation.

In life this can translate to trying to figure out where you will live, what type of work you will do, and who you will marry. Until you've had the experience firsthand, you do not know what the choices are. The contrast of knowing what you do want and what you don't want brings you closer to understanding yourself on a deeper level, and this, in turn gives you the courage to pursue your dreams and passions with enthusiasm.

In business this can be the period of time where you are figuring out what type of business model you wish to pursue. For me, making the jump from being an employee of the school district and a small business owner in real estate to becoming an online entrepreneur was definitely one of 'unconscious incompetence, where I did not even know which questions to ask until I had taken action on a few simple aspects of the business.

The next stage is that of conscious incompetence. You may not understand or know how to do something, but you recognize this fact, as well as the value of a new skill in addressing this deficit in your mind. The making of mistakes of all types and dimensions can be integral to the learning process at this stage.

When I was starting my business and getting involved with charities and fundraising I was aware of what I did not know and set out to educate myself through a variety of means. This can be a frustrating stage, but it needn't be if you stay focused on what is possible when you follow through and are able to move on to the next stage.

Next comes unconscious competence, where you are just beginning to master some skills but do not realize you have come so far. Someone might ask you a question on a topic you have been learning and while you are explaining it to them you will become aware of just how much you now know. One of my students recently experienced this while in Santa Barbara at my Retreat. Maria was explaining the process of marketing for small businesses to another of my students and they both realized simultaneously how far Maria had come in the months since they had seen each other at my workshop in Las Vegas. This can be quite an exciting feeling and lets you know that you are moving forward rapidly.

Finally, conscious competence takes over. You now know that you are completely competent within certain areas and aspects of your life and business and are able to make things move smoothly on a daily basis. Do not rest on your laurels here, as you must continue this cycle of the four stages if you are to truly transform your life. Allow yourself to let go of ego and control and be willing to submit to a lifetime of seeking knowledge and working to master it. Becoming a lifelong learner will serve you well over the years.

Every month you will want to revisit your goals by reviewing your Mission and Vision for your life and business. These may include goals for your health, wealth, family, and faith.

As Jack Canfield has taught for years, set a BHAG – a Big, Hairy, Audacious Goal – for yourself and then work to make it become a reality. My BHAGs have taken me far out of my comfort zone over these past several years. Be willing to accept that you will be unconsciously incompetent in the beginning, and that it is completely up to you to move to the next level as quickly as is comfortable for you and your agenda.

Getting Into the Habit of Transformation

Remember to take everything one step at a time. We can't transform our lives overnight, and probably wouldn't want to do that even if it were possible. I find that if I grow incrementally the changes are easier to adjust to and internalize. Instead of thinking about instantaneous change, think about getting into the habit of growth and change and of achieving a small success every single day. Everything you do moves you closer to your goals or further away from them, so develop habits that work in your favor. Before you know it, you will have reached your goals and will be setting new ones to achieve.

Your Dynamic 'To-Do' List

Don't depend on your memory to remember important tasks. They say that the dullest ink is better than the sharpest mind, and that is so true. Recently I spent several days in Austin speaking at a marketing event, where I made notes for myself each day on what I wanted to accomplish upon my return. When I got back to California I took out my list and did everything I had promised myself I would do. This included sending emails, packaging up and mailing two of my books, and more. I felt very productive because I did it all within a couple of hours of being back home, and did not rely on my memory at all.

Instead, I use something I refer to as a dynamic to-do list. This is a list of my thoughts, ideas, appointments, people I want to reach out to, blog post and short report ideas, and other goals that I keep on a mini legal pad (about five by eight inches in size). As I complete a task or delegate it to someone else I draw a line through it. When the page is filled I transfer the items that still need to be accomplished to a new page and save the old one in the back of the note pad. I have a box of these completed pads that go back to 2010, in case I want to look at them in the future to see how my goals have evolved.

This enables me to prioritize the tasks and activities in my life. I love the feeling of accomplishment when something is done and I draw that line through it. It's as though I have achieved a small success that I am celebrating. I add as many things as possible to this list before I turn off my computer each night, and the next morning I read through it as my computer is starting up. I also use a wall and desk calendar to have an overview of my week, month, and quarter. Being able to see the 'Big Picture' makes my goals more tangible in my mind. I'm fairly 'low tech' when it comes to this part of my life. Other than using Google Docs and the calendar on my iPhone, I use pen and paper to plan out and organize my life.

One thing I do now to be more productive is to take full responsibility for everything in my life, something I discussed earlier in this book. This was not the case while I was a classroom teacher and working in real estate. During that twenty year period I felt victimized by my situation and blamed others for what was occurring in my life. Now I look back and wonder why I ever lived this way and allowed that type of thinking to take over my daily life experience. Since coming online in 2006 I have assumed responsibility for my thoughts, actions, and results and have had incredible results.

I recommend you do the same and see what a huge difference it will make for you as you work towards your dreams and goals.

In my previous life I worked ten to twelve hours each day, six or seven days a week. This does not mean that I was productive for that many hours each day, as I personally do not believe this to be possible, except in rare circumstances when you are finishing a project or caught up in the excitement of what you are working on. Instead, strive for maximum productivity in just a few hours each day, preferably during your 'prime time' hours.

My most alert and productive hours are early in the morning, so I like to begin writing and creating products by seven each morning. These morning hours and my routine are non-negotiable. I end by ten or so, and am able to accomplish more during those three hours than I would if I sat in front of my computer for eight or ten hours each day. This is just how our brains are wired, so explore how and when you work best and adjust your schedule accordingly.

Time is not our enemy; time just is. Once you embrace the idea that time is on your side you will most definitely accomplish more, and in a more meaningful way each and every day. Focus on taking yourself more seriously and others around you will do the same. Ignore interruptions, for when you know what is important it's a whole lot easier to ignore what is not.

Sometimes my 'To-Do' list whittles away more slowly than at other times. It's not that I'm busy with family or other personal events; it's more that I just don't feel inspired at times and need to get away to think.

My Thoughts on Entrepreneurship

Starting a new business as an entrepreneur can be daunting, but if that is your goal then there has never been a better window of opportunity for success. Think about the exact type of business you want to create, the lifestyle you are dreaming of, and how this new venture will evolve over time. This will ensure that you are starting a business that will be rewarding and fulfilling over the years.

There are so many business models to choose from it's worth your time and effort to explore as many opportunities as possible. Many businesses, including mine, are run exclusively online. Others utilize a combination of online and offline strategies. You may also decide to start a service based business, rather than creating your own products or recommending those of an affiliate. Whatever your decision, know that the possibilities are almost endless.

Lifestyle is another consideration when you decide to become an entrepreneur. Many of the people I know prefer to work the days and times that suit them, based on their already busy lives and schedules. Others prefer to work Monday through Friday and have weekends and holidays to themselves to relax and spend time with family and friends. My business blurs the lines between business and pleasure and that suits me just fine.

Over time your business will change and transform, based on your experiences and ever changing goals. One morning you'll wake up and decide that you want to pursue an entirely different path from the one you have been on for awhile. This is all part of the process and you can look forward to the experiences and people you will encounter as this occurs.

I believe that the most important thing is to be fearless as an entrepreneur. During all of the years I worked as an employee I lived in fear of not meeting the school district's standards, of letting the administrators and other teachers down, and of not being the best employee I knew that I could be. I knew that I could be replaced very quickly, even after I had put in many years and had gained experience in my specialty. As an entrepreneur I please only myself, and the people who do business with me give me feedback as to what works best for them.

As our economy experiences full recovery after a devastating recession for the past five years or so, embrace the idea of entrepreneurship to see where it will take you. It may be the most lucrative and rewarding journey you have ever taken.

The above is an article I originally wrote for distribution to a niche directory. Feel free to use it as a post on your blog or as a part of a short report to get your own business up and running.

Why Is It So Different For Entrepreneurs?

Most of what I'm writing about here can be applied to any group of people, but some of it is directly geared at entrepreneurs, and more specifically to *online* entrepreneurs. As I shared at the beginning, we are a different breed who experience life in a unique way. No one is born an entrepreneur, yet some of us are drawn to this lifestyle at some point and for one or more of a variety of reasons.

Think back to when you were first toying with the idea of entrepreneurship as a life's calling. How did you picture what was possible? Did you even know what to expect or plan for?

I grew up around people who were, for the most part anyway, employees or independent contractors.

On Becoming a Transformational Entrepreneur

The idea of transforming your life and the lives of others around you with your entrepreneurial pursuits is not a new one. In fact, that's one of the reasons I was drawn to this life as an entrepreneur in the first place. I can remember having lunch with a friend during December of 2005 and telling her that I was going to get involved with helping charities with their fundraising and volunteering for all kinds of projects once my new online business got off the ground. She gave me a puzzled look but did not attempt to discourage me. I must have had conviction in my voice as I spoke.

She asked me if I knew how to do any of the things I was talking about, or if I knew of anyone personally living this type of lifestyle. I told her that I did not, but that many people were already doing this, I intended to meet them, and they would teach me how to get involved. This is indeed what happened, and now my life is filled with opportunities to serve others.

If you are a new entrepreneur, please understand this lifestyle is not without its challenges. Knowing that others have come before you and have overcome all of the challenges you have yet to discover is comforting, at least on the surface.

The term *transformational entrepreneur* is one which I use to describe the type of person who is willing to let go of the past and dive head first into the future. Part of this is a willingness to let go of most everything that has manifested previously in your life. This requires both confidence and trust. Confidence on a personal level that helps you to know you are capable of creating the future that you want in your life, and also the confidence to know that others will be there to support you throughout your process. Without this confidence you are unable to let go of what is currently in your life experience.

It may seem surprising that I haven't mentioned financial challenges until now, but they will be there. During my first year online I had to watch every penny. I had resigned from the school district and given away my real estate clients, so there was no money coming into my bank account. I had cashed out my retirement account with the State of California so I'd have money to live on that year, but it went much more quickly than I had budgeted for.

At one point my cell phone was shut off for non-payment and I considered getting part-time work as a substitute teacher. When that plan didn't pan out I realized it was for the best, and I returned to keeping my head down and getting to work with my online business. Being hungry (literally) for success gave me the inner strength to move forward with a focused sense of urgency.

Finding Your Passion

I'm excited, happy, and productive and this has manifested in my life as joyous and rewarding days that are extremely profitable as well. I truly believe this is all because I'm so passionate about what I do. Successful entrepreneurs are always passionate about what they do and how they serve others. And here's why that matters so much.

When you're passionate about something you will do it well. This goes back to our childhood when we believed anything was possible and followed our bliss. No matter what you pursue in your life, it is bound to be more successful if you love it. Also, when you do something well you become successful at it far more easily. When you're excelling at something, you enjoy it even more and that enjoyment makes you even more passionate. It's a 'catch-22' that works in your favor.

And so the circle continues because the passion for what you're doing grows and grows. Then you evolve and grow in your life's journey, too. Your life changes and new things are more important to you.

I get emails from so many people who say they're unsure of which niche to choose, are having difficulty coming up with ideas for products, and have very little confidence when it comes to reaching out to other entrepreneurs. I firmly believe it is because they are not passionate about what they are doing. Deep down inside they know there heart isn't in it and they are not ready to commit to following through.

Find your passion and the success and income will find you. Instead of your life being a struggle it will be fun and satisfying. You might not even know what you're passionate about until you go through the steps of deciding what it is you like to write about or create. Be willing to take the time to go through this process and choose wisely.

I can hear you now...

'But I'm not passionate about anything.'

Don't tell me you're not passionate about anything at all because I simply will not believe you. The opportunities for new entrepreneurs are endless. Find your passion and start building a life that will pay off handsomely in both joyous rewards and monetary rewards.

So, I will ask you once again...Are you passionate about what you're doing in your business right now? I believe that this makes a huge difference in the level of success you are able to achieve. Think about why you are doing the work you are involved in, how you can make it more fun and in alignment with your goals and dreams, and how you can slowly transition into the exact area you wish to work in over the next few months.

Most of us are working at jobs or running a business that we did not plan to be involved in. Life happens, and we find ourselves doing something for many years that we may have originally thought of as just something we would do for a short time. It wasn't until I was thirty years old that I went back to college to earn my teaching credential, and it took another twenty years before I realized I was no longer passionate about continuing with that work. Take a close look at what you are doing each day and determine if that is what you want to do forever.

Depending upon your circumstances you may not be in a position to leave your work and start something new overnight. In that case, look for ways to make it more fun and fulfilling. If I had stayed in education I would have returned to school to prepare for a more specialized position in the area of technology, something I had become quite passionate about over time. The work you want to do might be right under your nose if you take the time to seek out alternatives to your current position and job duties.

I spent two full years making my transition from classroom teacher to online entrepreneur, even though it appears that I did it overnight. Have a family meeting to discuss the alternatives and what that would look like for you and your family. Perhaps returning to school is the answer for you. Investigate and explore your options for starting a new local business or of becoming an online entrepreneur. Know that you can plan to change your working life completely and it will become a reality.

As you can see, caring deeply about what you do is important. Focus on your specific goals and then take the necessary steps to make it happen in your life as quickly as possible. Great success can be achieved when you move towards your passions.

The Transformational Entrepreneur's Pursuit of Happiness

The concept of happiness can be an interesting one. I think of it as a feeling of inner peace and joy in knowing that your life is in balance and the people you care about have what they want and need. But this feeling can be fleeting, as in the case of the new parent who goes from an almost euphoric state to one of panic and despair when the baby becomes ill.

So how can you be happy without an endless pursuit, and be satisfied with knowing that you control and are responsible for your own thoughts and feeling one hundred percent of the time?

Make some clear goals about what you want in your life and where you want to be. This could be around your work, your relationships, your health, or anything else that matters to you.

If something is not working for you, make a plan to make a change. Write down your thoughts on this in measurable terms. If we don't measure what isn't working we are unable to work towards a changing our situation for the better. Simply saying that you hate your job is not enough to get you into a new working environment. Write down what you like and dislike about where you are now and then brainstorm ideas as to how you can move forward over a specific period of time.

I think of this as the ongoing process of moving from complaining to actually solving your problem. It has to do with self-talk as well. Instead of complaining out loud or to yourself that you are broke or fat, try saying something like 'I am going to find a way to pay off ten thousand dollars of credit card debt over the next six months' or 'I am going to eliminate sugar from my diet for seven days as a way to begin my weight loss program'. Then brainstorm some ideas on how you can follow through and actively participate in the changes you want to experience.

We must take focused action on any goals we set for ourselves, and constantly ask yourself this question:

'Are my actions taking me closer to or
further away from my goals?'

A goal without a plan is just a wish, so be willing to move forward by taking massive action in the areas of your life you are working on right now and see how happy you are as you begin to accomplish even small steps towards your goals.

As an example of this strategy I will share that when I earned my first twenty-one dollars and sixty cents as an affiliate marketer back in 2006 I was overjoyed. It was such a tiny accomplishment, but it proved to me that my actions were working and that I could use the same methods and techniques to create an online empire. I did just that and continue to grow.

Now that you've set a goal for yourself, find a way to make it happen. I have a friend you wants to become a known and respected author in the science fiction genre, so let's use this as an example. Now that he knows exactly what he wants, he must create a plan to get from where he is right now to where he wants to be at a specific date in the future. He has decided this will take him one year.

His list of action during the first month might include:

- Reading two of the science fiction books that are already successful
- Research the authors and the publishing companies
- Making or revising an outline for his own book
- Connecting with a local writer's group for this genre, or start his own group
- Schedule time every single day to write and to do the other things on this list

- Committing to write one short story in the science fiction genre every month and sending it to magazines to be published

I told him that he must make a seven day a week commitment to this goal for the next three hundred and sixty-five days if he expects to achieve the greatest success. The example I used was caring for a pet. We don't skip a day in feeding, walking, or petting our dog because we didn't have the time. We make the time for what we want to accomplish, every single time.

Surrounding yourself with the right people is crucial to your success. Get rid of the negative, complaining, and unkind people you may be currently allowing into your life. Replace them with positive, uplifting, and kind people who will champion your efforts to transform your life. Whomever we choose to spend time with will affect our state of mind, and our results so choose wisely. You deserve to have the most positive and useful thoughts filling your subconscious mind.

Where do these positive people congregate? Online they will be in groups and forums and offline they will be in Meetup groups and service organizations. Spend time finding them and then become a part of the groups that feel right for you. If you want a better life, first create the mindset that you deserve it and then find the people who will support you and your ideas and dreams.

It's so much easier to let life just happen to you, instead of actively doing the work to make things better. Don't allow this to happen to you! Create meaningful goals, surround yourself with positive influences, and know that you can do anything you want with your life. See the glass as half full and take appropriate actions every single day. We receive whatever we believe throughout our lifetimes.

There is a concept referred to as 'upper limiting', where we begin to sabotage ourselves when things feel too good or our success is greater than we have previously experienced in our lives. Deep down we are afraid that we won't be able to handle the new changes and feelings so we seek to stop the success in its tracks. Change in any form can be scary. If you start getting sick more often, becoming disagreeable around other people, or just feeling out of sorts generally, upper limiting could be the culprit. Accept it and then step back from your situation to see that you deserve everything wonderful that's coming your way.

Don't wait for the perfect conditions to appear. There will never be a better time or better circumstances than are present at this exact point in time. Believe that and keep moving forward. Don't feel like something has to occur first before you can take action. Start from wherever you are and know that it's in perfect alignment with your dreams and goals. Gratitude is still the fastest path to multiplying your blessings exponentially.

Never feel like it is too late or that you are too old to get started and transform your life. As my friend Craig Ballantyne, editor of Early to Rise says, 'Age is just a number. You can transform your life at ANY age.' I was almost fifty when I made the conscious decision to change my life completely, and during these past nine years I've felt younger than ever as I continue to transform my thoughts, ideas, actions, and results.

Accountability - To Yourself And to Others

Many of us have difficulty with managing our time effectively, discerning between urgent, high priority tasks and those that can wait or be delegated to others, and sabotaging our own efforts on a regular basis. If this describes you, then accountability is an area you'll want to get involved in.

The most gifted accountability coach I know is Debbie O'Grady. She makes the entire process a seamless one. I have learned from her that my actions either lead me closer to my goals or further away from them. She also teaches about procrastination and other time wasters that sneak into your daily life. Debbie also provides you with the tools to understand the direction your actions will take you and teach you how to forecast the results so you know which road to walk in the future. I've learned from her how to create the most efficient and effective direction to produce the biggest results. You can be sure that you will develop a clear mindset of what works and what doesn't when you are accountable.

When I was first starting out I had many 'limiting beliefs' about what I could or could not achieve in my life. Being accountable to Mentors as well as to myself changed all of that. When I redefined how I approached my personal and professional goals I understood that I could achieve anything I set my mind to do.

Write down your dreams and goals, set priorities for what you wish to accomplish, and then be accountable for achieving what you want in a specific and defined time frame. You will amaze yourself as you transform into the person you were meant to be.

Leveraging Other People's Time

There are so many ways to transform your business exponentially and we will explore some of the possibilities in this section.

- Outsourcing - If someone else can do something I don't know how to do or don't like to do, especially if they work by the hour or by the project, then I am going to outsource it almost immediately. In the beginning you may feel like you can't afford to pay other people to help you, but once you give it a try I predict that you'll see the benefit almost immediately.

- Joint Venture Partnerships - Start connecting with people as soon as possible to see how you can help each other move forward. This can double, triple, or even quadruple your reach. When you meet with people you like, whether it is in person or online find out how you can serve them. Align yourself with others, especially if they are your direct competition and everyone will benefit.

- Delegation - I shared earlier in the book how one of my students taught me the power of delegation years ago while I was a classroom teacher. I have now become somewhat of an expert when it comes to asking others to do things for me. These include both paid and gratis requests and I always reciprocate in some way. Once you get good at this there will be no stopping your growth.

Leveraging the time and expertise of others will fast track your business and personal success. Our goal as transformational entrepreneurs is to have time and financial freedom to serve others and lead the life we deserve.

Addendum

My life has been transformed over the past several years due in part to the business I have created. I am able to serve others who want to live the Internet lifestyle and work from home or from wherever they want to be. As you read this book you may have been thinking that you would like to do the same thing, or something similar.

On the following pages you will find a short report I wrote and use as a free giveaway for one of my sites, http://OnlineEntrepreneurBlueprint.com. In it I share and explain eleven distinct steps to achieving success as an online entrepreneur.

As you read through this report, please note several things.

- I utilize the concept of storytelling throughout the report, helping readers to know and identify with me.
- I keep the information simple and easy to understand and implement.
- Each step builds on the one previous, making for an organized approach.
- My affiliate links to the products and services I recommend are included.
- I include a 'Call to Action' at the end of the report so that readers may further engage me if they want to know more.

Read through this a couple of times and then commit to writing your own report to give away to the people in your target audience who may be interested in connecting with you in the future.

Your Online Entrepreneur Blueprint

11 Steps To Entrepreneurial Success

By Connie Ragen Green

What does it take to become a successful online entrepreneur today?

That's the question I am often asked, and I feel uniquely qualified to answer it in great detail for you.

My name is Connie Ragen Green, and I first came online at the end of 2005. I had been working for most of the previous 20 years as a classroom teacher in the Los Angeles area, teaching all the way from Kindergarten through high school. My favorite grades to teach were 5th and 6th, because I felt like I related to that age group in a special way. They were at the point in their lives where they needed an adult role model to help guide them to their future. Also, they 'got' my jokes, allowing for an open learning environment in which young minds could receive knowledge and expand.

At the same time I was also working as a real estate broker and residential appraiser. I did this after school, on weekends, and during school breaks and vacations. I had worked in real estate for several years in my 20s before returning to school to earn my teaching credential, and loved helping people to find a new home or sell the one they had, and to receive a fair price for it. The additional income was also important to me, as everyone knows that school teachers do not earn enough money to buy a home, especially in southern California. My appraisal work took me from my home at that time in the San Fernando Valley section of Los Angeles to as far south as San Diego, east to Palm Springs, and as far north as Santa Barbara, and even further at times. Sometimes I would put a thousand miles on my car within the course of a single week.

By 2005 I was exhausted from working six or seven days a week for the past twenty years, with only a few short real vacations during that time. Perhaps the most difficult part of these was that I was still living month to month, with no hope of getting ahead financially. I'm also a cancer survivor, so I knew that my life had to hold more meaning than to simply spend it working at jobs I no longer had a passion for. When I discovered that people were making a living on the Internet with information products, affiliate marketing, and online training I knew this was for me.

The question I had to ask myself was this: "Am I willing to do what it takes to become an online entrepreneur?"

That was in December of 2005. I set about to see if I could start an online business, or if this was something others could be successful at but not me. My belief system at that time included the feeling that everyone else was smarter than I was, had a stronger background in whatever I was trying to achieve, and simply knew things that I did not. Over the next six months to a year I was tested time and time again as I worked hard to put the pieces in place. There was no boss or supervisor checking to see what I had done each day. I earned no money in the very beginning, yet I was having to spend money on domains, web hosting, the teleseminar service, and an autoresponder account. Would it all be worth it?

The answer was a resounding Yes! And now I teach others how to get started with their own Internet businesses.

Becoming an entrepreneur of any type is simply not for everyone. If you are used to having a traditional schedule, weekends off, and a regular paycheck you may not care for having your own business. If, on the other hand, you look forward to being in charge and making decisions, having the opportunity to earn as much as you want to, and love taking risks on a daily basis, entrepreneurship could be exactly what suits you best.

In order to build up a successful business online you must be willing to do what it takes. This means setting up a quiet workspace for yourself at home, scheduling the days and times you will be at work, creating content for your blog and websites, and connecting with others both online and in person. Of course, this is after you have chosen a niche in which to specialize and made sure it is one that will hold your interest for at least the next year. I'll be going into great detail with each of these areas when we discuss the 11 steps to entrepreneurial success.

You must also find out what your competition is already selling to this market. Competition is to be respected because this means that people are ready, willing, and able to spend money on a variety of products and services. Join the list of everyone who is currently serving your market to see what they have to say, and become an affiliate for them if they have such a program.

Now it is time for you to make a name for yourself in your chosen niche. Blog as often as possible and say what you think. It's better to be controversial and speak your mind than to be wishy-washy and go along with everyone else. Read everything you can on your topic, and not just from online sources. Visit your public library and bookstores. See what you already may have on your bookshelves at home. Focus on becoming as knowledgeable as you possibly can on your niche topic, as this is the path to becoming an expert or authority.

The final piece is marketing your new online business, and that's the glue to keeping it all together. I like to market every single day, even weekends and holidays because it makes my business stronger and increases my income. Remember that a single tweet on Twitter is marketing, and that much of your online marketing can be automated, so it's not like you'll be sitting in front of your computer six or seven days a week.

Have fun with the marketing and it will serve you well. Send out email messages to the people who join your list, including links to your blog posts, affiliate offers, and excellent resources. Be active on the 'Big Three' social media sites (Facebook, Twitter, and LinkedIn) and share your blog posts and other content there as well. It won't be long before you are thought of as an authority in your niche, and your online business begins to skyrocket. Doing what it takes is your key to success.

As I stated earlier, it took me almost a year to start making a decent amount of money online. I had made a few hundred dollars during the first six months, but it was hit and miss and barely paid my expenses for hosting, autoresponders, and domains. I believe it was due to the fact that I did not have the 11 steps I will be sharing with you here in place in my own online business. If I had known then what I know now, things would have been very different.

Instead of taking 18 months to replace my offline income, I could have done it in 6 to 9 months. I have included the 11 steps to starting your online business in the order they should be done. You can do this in as little as thirty days, but most people will spend at least two to three months to get started. Take it at your own pace, and don't omit any steps.

Let's get started!

11 Steps To Entrepreneurial Success Based on My Experience and Those Of My Own Students

Step #1 – Change Your Mindset

Thinking about your life is a matter of choice. Earlier I said that my belief system before I became an entrepreneur included the feeling that everyone else was smarter than I was, had a stronger background in whatever I was trying to achieve, and simply knew things that I did not. It took time for me to understand there was no truth in that whatsoever. Know that you are capable of great things and that you can activate that part of your mind's thinking at any time.

I used to engage in negative self-talk every single day of my life. Once I began to focus on the positive aspects of who I was I could look into the mirror every morning and say something to the effect of 'You are smart and have knowledge and information that will change other people's lives forever.' Now I can't imagine not feeling empowered in this way, but it did take some time to get to this point in my life. Being positive will meet with some resistance from those in your life you are steeped in negativity and self-doubt, but do not allow them to dictate your future. Practice positive self-talk every day and you will be amazed at the results.

Step #2 – Choose A Profitable Niche

Deciding what you have to offer others is sometimes the most difficult step of all. My advice is to choose an area you are interested in and know something about, and then jump in and get started. You may find that the first niche you choose does not hold your interest forever, but you must begin somewhere in order to get started with this process. Take a close look at your work experience in previous years, hobbies, and other areas of interest to you.

This is my 3 circle Venn diagram that you might remember from school. I use it to help my coaching clients choose a niche that is right for them. Recently I worked with someone who is an embroidery coach. She's been involved in embroidery since she was very young, and knows quite a bit about this topic. When we worked on this together she saw that she is passionate about helping others to start and grow an embroidery business, has lots of life experience in this area, and the market is definitely in place. Tens of thousands of people around the world are into embroidery, or want to get started with it. She is now on her way to online success and has already achieved great things.

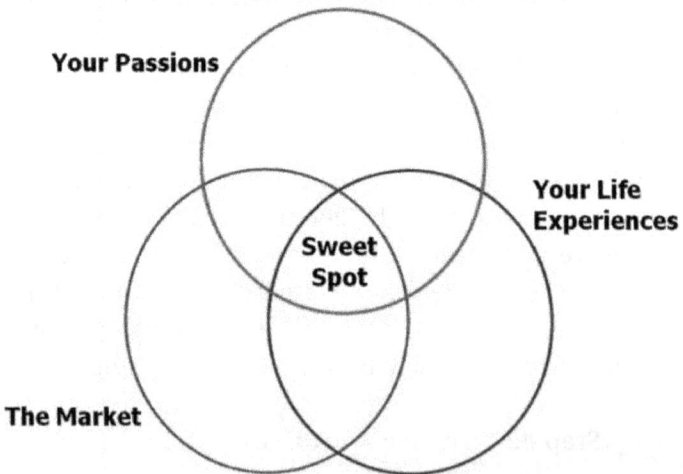

Your Passions

Your Life Experiences

Sweet Spot

The Market

Some of the most popular niches include:
- Health and Fitness
- Relationships
- Make Money/Save Time
- DIY Home Improvement
- Sports/Hobbies
- Family/Lifestyle/Choices
- Self Improvement/Personal Growth
- Becoming an Author

These are just a few examples of where you may want to start out with your online business.

Step #3 - Choose A Profitable Business Model

I have had up to eight streams of online income since starting my business at the beginning of 2006. These days I focus on just a few of these, but I wanted to make sure you knew about every possible way to earn money as an online entrepreneur. These business models include:

- Services – Take a look at the skills you have previously acquired, what you already know how to do, and which of these can be done from home. This could include transcribing, editing, setting up websites, graphic design, customer service, being a virtual assistant for one or more people, and more. You will find that there are thousands of people like myself who hire independent contractors to help us with our businesses. I have a dozen people who assist me in some capacity, and they are an integral part of my team. Being in service can be a lucrative and rewarding way to get started as an online entrepreneur.
- Local Business Marketing – I kind of fell into this business model by offering to help a family member

who had just started a handyman business. He was spending so much money on newspaper and magazine advertising that it would take him a couple of weeks each month just to get to the 'break even' point. I offered to help him in 2006 by using a blog and other online marketing techniques I was learning and within two months he had dropped the other advertising completely because he was getting so many calls.

Soon my insurance agent and dentist asked me to help them with their local marketing and on my way to a live event the following year I met two plumbers who hired me while we were at thirty thousand feet in the air! This continues to be an excellent business model.

- Affiliate Marketing – This is the process of recommending other people's products and services in return for a commission. Affiliate marketing continues to account for about half of my income each month, and I only recommend what I have purchased, consumed, and benefited from. I even wrote a book about it called *Huge Profits With Affiliate Marketing: How to Build an Online Empire by Recommending What You Love.* I go into much greater detail with all of the ways you can build a profitable business by being an affiliate for others.
- Information Product Creation – Creating your own line of products will serve you well over time. I started with simple courses that consisted of three or four live teleseminars with recordings, transcripts, and Study Guides. Other products consist of a written guide in PDF (portable document format) and a few short videos. These courses become evergreen products you can sell online for years to come. You then set up an affiliate program so that others can promote you and

your products the way you do when you are the affiliate.

Keep your products simple and create them as quickly as possible for best results. A great example of this is a course that I created with one of my students, Adrienne Dupree. It's at http://TopWPPluginsForBusiness.com and is only $7.

- Membership Sites – Everyone loves to feel like they belong to a group, so you can set up membership sites to include your products and other information. Then you sell a monthly, annual, or lifetime subscription to your site and continue to add to your training as you bring in new members. This has become super simple in recent years thanks to an inexpensive plugin for WordPress called Wishlist. I now have many membership sites of all kinds and find it to be the easiest way to increase my income while building my online business. You can find out more about the Wishlist plugin at http://ConnieLoves.me/Wishlist.
- Niche Sites – If you're truly having fun with your Internet business then you'll want to expand into other niches for fun and profit. This is where I first began including close friends and family members in what I was doing online. Choose topics of interest like cooking, skateboarding, or travel and set up a simple WordPress site. There's an entire strategy to this that includes using PLR (private label rights) content and promoting products through an affiliate link for Amazon, Clickbank, or other programs and even adding some AdSense blocks to further monetize your site.
- Authorship/Speaking/Consulting – I didn't even think of this as a business model until I wrote my first book in 2010. Even though I had been speaking at marketing events for a couple of years by then it was

when I was first published that I saw the lucrative possibilities of writing, speaking, and consulting. You can see how I've done this by visiting my Author's Page on Amazon at http://ConnieRagenGreenBooks.com.

- Coaching/Mentoring – I highly recommend that you achieve some success yourself before offering to help others. You want to have a certain level of credibility, and I waited until I had reached six figures a year at the end of 2007 before starting my Mentor Program. This accounts for only about ten percent of my overall income because my time is precious and I prefer to work with fewer people on a one to one basis.

By now you can see that there are quite a few business models to pursue as an online entrepreneur. Start with one or two to begin with and see where that strategy leads you.

Step #4 Purchase Your Domains And Hosting

Next, you will want to purchase your domain names and hosting. If you do not yet have your name as a dot come, as I do with both ConnieGreen.com and ConnieRagenGreen.com, do that first. If your name is not available you'll want to choose a middle name or initial to claim your name online. Someone had ConnieGreen.com already when I got started, so I put a backorder on it and was able to pick it up the following year. This will be the most important domain you own, so purchase it for five years or longer.

Your other sites will need their own domains. Start with one other one to set up your business. Choose a domain name that says what you will be doing online. Remember that you are just starting out, so don't worry about choosing the perfect domain name. Shorter is better – three or four words – and you will be better off with a .com than with any other extension.

Your domain must live somewhere so that you can quickly install a WordPress site. For hosting, I recommend http://BlueHostSolutions.com (this is my affiliate link). This is what is referred to as C-panel hosting, and this service allows you to add Wordpress in just a few clicks so that you will be ready to start blogging. The cost for this is less than one hundred dollars for an entire year. You can have up to 100 domains with just one account, so it is extremely cost effective. I do NOT recommend using GoDaddy for your hosting because they are not equipped with C-panel and you will run into problems almost immediately as you start your online business.

Step #5 – Set Up A WordPress Blog/Site

When I was just starting out, Wordpress seemed too confusing for me. It was very technical. Now it is much easier to do because it has become user friendly. You will install Wordpress on your domain with just a few clicks through your hosting account.

Now you will want to add a new theme to your blog. In Wordpress the theme is just a 'skin', meaning that you can change your theme at any time and your content will remain intact.

Add an optin box – You will want people to leave their name and email address when they visit your blog. This is accomplished by adding an optin box in the upper right hand corner of your site. You will need an autoresponder service in order to do this. There are several choices for this. Right now I am recommending that you get started with a service called Aweber (my link is http://ConnieLoves.me/Aweber) This includes tutorials and customer service to help you get set up. They also generate the html code you will need, enabling you to simply copy and paste what you need. It's only one dollar for the first month when you sign up using my link, and

$19/month thereafter. If you pay quarterly or annually you'll save some money as well.

Step #6 - Create A Free Giveaway

When someone visits your blog, your goal is to interest them enough for them to want to leave their name and email address. The way to do this is by giving them a free gift on your topic. This can be a one page checklist, 10 tips on how to do what you teach, an audio recording, a short video, or a short report. Keep your free gift short and to the point. Remember that this is only to give your prospects a taste of what you have to offer, and to show them that you do have information on your topic that will be valuable to them over time.

What you are reading right now is a short report I put together for those opting in to my newest site. I can then repurpose this content into a variety of different formats, helping people around the globe in the process.

Step #7 - Choose Three Affiliate Products To Promote

Before I ever had my own product I was promoting affiliate products. This enabled me to see how the process of buying and selling on the Internet really worked, and also gave me some income as I was learning what I needed to do. You can find digital products to sell in a variety of places, including Clickbank and JVZoo. You have also most likely purchased products and courses that you can promote as an affiliate.

On Clickbank – http://Clickbank.com - they will ask you to create a nickname to use for your account. This should be just a short name, using letters and numbers if you like, that will give you your unique name on Clickbank. I recommend not using your name, even though you will mask this link so no one will see it anyway. Clickbank is home to more than

25K digital products, in a wide variety of niches. They will pay you every two weeks once you have met the initial requirements as spelled out in their TOS (terms of service).

I have found it difficult to find the exact products I need on Clickbank, so I recommend a site called http://ClickbankProSearch.com as a way to search by keyword for what you want to promote to your prospects. This is a paid site, but you can get a 15 day free trial to see how it works. I am there almost every week to find new products to promote and to do my research for new products I will create.

JV Zoo is a newer site that has grown exponentially in the past year. You can not only find products to promote here but also sell your own product through their affiliate program. Take a look at http://ConnieLoves.me/JVZoo to get started.

Now take a look at the products and services you've already purchased online. Most of them will offer an affiliate program, so look for one that fits your niche and sign up as an affiliate. My advice is to only promote three products during your first two or three months of setting up your business. This will keep you focused so you can start making some money and see how this business works. By doing so, you will gain greater insight into how you want to develop your business and what your 'Big Picture' goals will be.

I believe it is important to point out here that you should only promote the products and services you have purchased yourself. You are building your reputation online, and you don't want someone to see that you are promoting their product, service, or training course when you haven't purchased it and benefitted from it yourself. That's the fastest way to lose credibility, and you don't want that to happen. Instead, make the decision to only recommend what you love!

Step #8 - Become a Content Creation Machine

Content creation is at the basis of everything we do online. Whether it be written, spoken, or video our messages must reach our prospects and clients in some format. We typically start writing first, and then move on to audio recordings and videos. Begin by posting to your blog and writing articles regularly. This gives your readers a better idea of who you are and what you stand for. This will take the most time on your part, but it is absolutely crucial to your initial success.

My writing was horrible for the first few months, and it would take me about two hours to write an article or a blog post. Within a couple of months it all got faster and easier, like everything in our life does with practice and now I am able to write and submit an article in about thirty minutes. I use http://EzineArticles.com as my main site to submit my articles. I have been with this site since 2007. You can see how many articles I currently have there by going to my expert bio page at http://ArticlesByConnieRagenGreen.com.

Repurpose your articles into blog posts and short reports. Soon you will find that just one article can be used in many different ways, including turning that content into teleseminars and the basis of your own product. Repurposing is the way you can take just one simple idea and turn it into massive content and products of your own.

Hosting your own teleseminars will jumpstart your business. As soon as possible, let people hear your voice. This makes a huge difference in how quickly you can build your business online. As soon as I started holding a free call every week, more people began to join my list and buy things that I recommended. I want to invite you to hear my latest teleseminar by going to http://AskConnieAnything.com. Sign up for a 21 day trial of the program I've been using for this since 2007 for only $1 at http://TeleseminarStrategies.com

Video is also an excellent way to create content quickly. I still use a Flip camera for all of my videos, but those are no longer made. Instead, go over to Amazon and see the ones you can get for under a hundred dollars at http://ConnieLoves.me/Kodak. I also have my own Channel over at YouTube where you can subscribe at http://YouTube.com/ConnieRagenGreen.

Step #9 - Get Social!

Social media has made it so much easier to get started with an online business than ever before. There was no social media at all during my first year online, and it took another year for it to catch on. You can connect with people who are interested in your topic, and begin to invite them to your blog and to join your list. The 'Big 3' of social media are Twitter, Facebook, and LinkedIn. If you haven't already, go to these sites and claim your name.

Follow me on Twitter by going to http://twitter.com/conniegreen and introduce yourself. Join Facebook and set up your profile. My personal page is at http://facebook.com/ConnieRagenGreen. Join LinkedIn and fill out the information they ask for initially. I'm Connie Ragen Green there as well and you can connect with me at http://www.linkedin.com/in/ConnieRagenGreen. All of these sites will become part of what you do to attract prospects into your business. Just get started now and it will all fall into place over time. Social media can become a huge time waster, so limit yourself to a maximum of thirty minutes a day when you are just starting out, and fifteen to twenty minutes a day as you become more proficient. My motto is 'Get in, get out, and get back to work!' This is also something that can be easily outsourced once you have everything set up initially.

Step #10 – Connect with others for Masterminding and Joint Ventures

My one regret with my own business is that I did not begin connecting your other entrepreneurs much sooner.

Instead I stayed home, working at my computer for hours at a time and convincing myself it just wasn't time for me to meet others face to face. Once I took that step in 2008 and began meeting other like-minded individuals my business took off in a huge way. I met people who were both new and filled with great ideas, as well as those who had been working online for ten years already.

Attending live events is the best way to connect with entrepreneurs in person and there are two events I speak at regularly that attract people in every niche you can imagine. One is Dennis Becker's Earn 1K a Day event held each summer, and the best way to get connected with Dennis is by going to http://ConnieLoves.me/WhatHappens and downloading the eBook that chronicles a recent event.

The other event I speak at twice each year is NAMS – the Novice to Advanced Marketing Seminar. You can get started with the free weekly trainings and see how this group could make a difference for you. It's at http://ConnieLoves.me/NAMSWeekly.

I also host my own live events, so if you have joined my list you will hear more about them over time.

I have been provided with many opportunities by attending live events, and would love to meet you in person at one of them.

Step #11 - Your Own Information Products

As soon as you decide that you will stick with your chosen niche for *at least* the next six months, think about a product you will create. You can write a short report, such as I have done here, and sell it for anywhere from $7 to $17. You can then add an audio recording of you reading the report and that could sell for $27. I recommend creating an inexpensive product to begin with, just to understand how the process works. The best training you will receive on how to do this successfully is my comprehensive program at:

http://WriteShortReports.com. This is training on a brilliant strategy for creating short report products on your niche topic that your prospects will pay for. Use the code word *PROFIT* to bring it down from the regular price of $37 to only $7.

Remember to keep it simple and include as much detailed information as possible so that you can continue to build your credibility in your niche.

I will recap these eleven steps for you again. They are:
1. Change Your Mindset
2. Choose A Niche
3. Choose A Business Model
4. Purchase Your Domains And Hosting
5. Set Up A Wordpress Blog And Optin
6. Create A Free Giveaway
7. Choose 3 Affiliate Products To Promote
8. Create Content
9. Connect On The 'Big 3' Social Media Sites
10. Connect With Others For Masterminding And Joint Ventures
11. Create Your Own Product

I have oversimplified many things I have included here in this report, but you definitely have enough information to start building your business. The purpose in doing that was to get you to take action quickly without having to think about too many things that can be better addressed down the line. There will be plenty of time to learn the more advanced strategies and techniques of online marketing. For now, just think about going through each of the 11 steps and doing something to start setting the wheels in motion for your future.

Find out more about me and what I am doing at my main site – http://HugeProfitsTinyList.com. You will be able to join my list and also get your free subscription to my popular podcast series.

To Your Massive Online Success!

Connie Ragen Green

RESOURCES

I have recommended quite a few excellent resources in this report. Please know that I do not recommend any person, product, or service lightly and that I use and benefit from everything I recommend. Many of these are my affiliate links, meaning that I will receive a commission when you make a purchase. You do not pay any more by going through someone's affiliate link, and many times you are being offered a bonus because of it. This is also one of the best ways for you to start earning money online.

Top 20 WordPress Plugins:
http://TopWPPluginsForBusiness.com

Membership Site Plugin:
http://ConnieLoves.me/Wishlist

My published books:
http://ConnieRagenGreenBooks.com

Autoresponder Services –
http://ConnieLoves.me/Aweber
My link gives you a $1 trial for the first month.

Domains – http://ConnieLoves.me/DomainSale
I purchase all of my domains at GoDaddy because of their excellent customer service and expertise in this area.

Hosting: http://BlueHostSolutions.com

Choose affiliate products: http://Clickbank.com and http://ConnieLoves.me/JVZoo

My published articles:
http://ArticlesByConnieRagenGreen.com

The Earn 1K a Day group:
http://ConnieLoves.me/WhatHappens

NAMS – Novice to Advanced Marketing group:
http://ConnieLoves.me/NAMSWeekly

Create a simple product: http://WriteShortReports.com
Use the code *PROFIT* to bring it down to only $7

Listen to my latest teleseminar at
http://AskConnieAnything.com

Sign up for a 21 day $1 trial to host your own calls at
http://TeleseminarStrategies.com

Inexpensive video cameras:
http://ConnieLoves.me/Kodak

My Channel on YouTube:
http://YouTube.com/ConnieRagenGreen

DISCLAIMER: I am an affiliate marketer and regularly recommend the products and services I am using in my own online business. I will receive a commission if you purchase these products or services through the links included in this report. I have used or currently continue to use each one I mention here and they each receive my 'Green Seal of Approval'.

To Your Massive Online Success!
Connie Ragen Green

Learn more about living the Internet lifestyle from my latest book, available at: http://ConnieLoves.me/Lifestyle

As you can see from reading this report, sharing your unique knowledge, experience, and perspective on your topic with others in your target audience gives you the opportunity to serve them. I'd love to know more about what you come up with, so do not hesitate to contact me through the site I have set up for this book at:

http://TheTransformationalEntrepreneur.com

Afterword

Now that you're read this book through for the first time, are you ready to begin your own transformation? Do you feel empowered, confident, and worthy of reaching for this level of enlightenment in your life and business? I hope so, because you sincerely deserve it, and more.

You may want to begin slowly as you reread this book. Perhaps you'll even call it something else, such as a revolution, an overhaul, a remodeling, radical change, reshaping, redoing, rearrangement, reworking, rejuvenating, revamping, or even a morphing of who you once were into who you want to be.

As you could tell as you made your way through the book, transformation requires, and even demands great change on a very personal level. Let go of your past and jump head first into your future as soon as possible for maximum effects. If you simply dip your toe into the water, your results will be mediocre at best.

I know way too many people who continue to live in the past and expect their lives to change for the better and move them forward. One man is a self-described 'hippy' from the last millennium who still has hair down to his waist. His clothing continues to reflect the days when you could wear an old t-shirt to a business meeting.

The result is that he is not taken seriously by the people he wishes to serve. I heard him speak about wanting to be successful without having to change who he is, but that simply is not possible. Of course, you will retain the values and beliefs you hold in your heart to be true, but in every other way you must grow and evolve to be current and contemporary. Look in the mirror, then ask the people you know, like, and trust to give you an honest assessment of what they see.

Another woman I know continues to talk about her children as though they were still in grammar school, yet they are married with children of their own now. She is also living in the past and not understanding why her life isn't more like what she dreamed of for so long.

Long ago we had a new principal at the second school I taught at who insisted we all dress like professionals. Back then I wore tennis shoes because I wanted to be comfortable. Many of the other teachers and I refused to give up our comfortable clothes and old ways of doing things. Now I know she was so right about this and other things. If I had only been willing to make an adjustment to my shoe choice I would have been perceived differently by those I wished to serve.

My wish for you is that you would come to your own conclusions about what will work best for your life.

It takes a village to create the life of your dreams. Thank you for allowing me to be a part of your village as you make the choices that will work for you in your life and business transformation.

I will leave you with a quote often credited to Steve Jobs in error; it was in fact written by advertising executive Rob Siltanen for Apple in the summer of 1997. The content is based on an original idea by art director and creative talent Craig Tanimoto and spoken by actor Richard Dreyfus. It was known as the 'Think Different' campaign. Siltanen had hoped that Robin Williams, a personal friend of Steve Jobs, would provide the voiceover, but Williams refused to do any advertising.

'Here's to the crazy ones. The misfits. The rebels. The troublemakers. The round pegs in the square holes. The ones who see things differently. They're not fond of rules. And they have no respect for the status quo. You can quote them, disagree with them, glorify or vilify them. But the only thing you can't do is ignore them. Because they change things. They push the human race forward. And while some may see them as the crazy ones, we see genius. Because the people who are crazy enough to think they can change the world, are the ones who do.'

If you believe you can become a transformational entrepreneur by changing your thoughts and actions, and are willing to take on the work required then you will most definitely achieve your goals.

Resources

Connie Ragen Green's main sites:
http://ConnieRagenGreen.com
http://HugeProfitsTinyList.com
http://TheTransformationalEntrepreneur.com

Forbes article on the 'Think Different' campaign for Apple:
http://www.forbes.com/sites/onmarketing/2011/12/14/the
-real-story-behind-apples-think-different-campaign

The Pomodoro Technique:
http://en.wikipedia.org/wiki/Pomodoro_Technique

Pamela Slim's TedX Talk:
https://www.youtube.com/watch?v=84QspUpX0b0

About the Author

Connie Ragen Green is a bestselling author of more than ten books, an international speaker, and an online marketing strategist who first took the Internet by storm in 2006 as an affiliate marketer. She makes her home in southern California, dividing her time between Santa Clarita in the desert and Santa Barbara at the beach.

Teaching others how to get started online and create a profitable business is Connie's passion and life's work. She is dedicated to the concept of helping others live the life they are dreaming of and deserve.

Connie has now spoken on three continents and has students all around the world. She continues to volunteer and participate actively in a variety of charitable organizations, including Rotary, Zonta, Elk's, and is supportive of many others, including the Boy's and Girl's Clubs, See International, and Carousel Ranch.

www.ingramcontent.com/pod-product-compliance
Lightning Source LLC
Chambersburg PA
CBHW060612200326
41521CB00007B/756